ADVANCE PRAISE FOR HUSTLE

"An important book that will show you how to build the bridge
between your potential and the opportunities that are waiting for you—if you
choose to go after them."
—*Bernadette Jiwa, bestselling author of* Meaningful *and* Difference

"If Love Is the Killer App, *Hustle* is its operating system. Read this book
and drive exponential success, starting today!"
—*Tim Sanders, bestselling author of* Love Is the Killer App *and* Dealstorming

"Why follow the herd and force yourself to fit into 'their system'
when you don't have to? Instead, use this book to hustle your own way
to success. On YOUR terms."
—*Claire Diaz-Ortiz, author and entrepreneur*

"What's the best way from Point A to Point B? Wrong question.
Read Patrick's book to discover why the best hustlers always succeed
by working backward from Point B to Point A."
—*Eric M. Jackson, author of* The PayPal Wars

"All you have to do is hustle . . . you hear it all the time. It's a trendy word
where the action related to it is easier said than done.
Here's a reference guide to make hustling productive and actionable."
—*Brian Solis, digital analyst, anthropologist, and bestselling author of*
X: The Experience When Business Meets Design

"Sometimes we all fall into a Cycle of Suck, where our talents remain obscured
behind a wall of misfortune. And that is precisely when you need to get off your
ass and hustle, unearth hidden opportunities, and change your life.
This book will tell you how to recharge your life with more money, meaning, and,
perhaps most important of all, momentum. Read it. You'll be glad you did."
—*Adam L. Penenberg, journalism professor at New York University
and author of* Viral Loop

"If I had the insights of *Hustle* <u>before</u> I became an entrepreneur, I would have a lot
less sleepless nights. Powerful, promising, and practical."
—*Sunni Brown, chief human potentialist and bestselling author of*
Gamestorming *and* The Doodle Revolution

"In life, you have no choice but to hustle—to pursue that which feeds your spirit and fulfills your dreams. This book is a must-read."
—*Pat Hiban, New York Times bestselling author of 6 Steps to 7 Figures, serial entrepreneur, and philanthropist*

"In the near future, algorithms will tell us what to do. They'll choose the safest, the best, the most predictable life. But inspiration and greatness is found on the road less taken—and that's why you need this book. Neil, Patrick, and Jonas show you, with powerful examples and concrete tools, how a blend of subversiveness, creativity, and simple grit can get you to your dreams. This should be on the bookshelf of everyone who has an idea that keeps them up at night."
—*Alistair Croll, entrepreneur and coauthor of* Lean Analytics

"Even amidst the chaos of the world, there's more opportunity than ever to succeed. The traditional ways of doing so (get a job, stay in it, retire comfortably) are being actively disrupted faster than ever before, which means we need a new framework for winning. *Hustle* is that framework."
—*Benjamin Yoskovitz, coauthor of* Lean Analytics

"Hustle is the blueprint I followed to land three dream jobs in a row. Stop trying to convince people to hire you, and show them what you can do."
—*Charlie Hoehn, author of* Play It Away

"Tired of looking at other people winning and thinking they are just lucky or come from privilege? Turns out that they actually have a different key ingredient in common: They hustle. Read this book and create your own blueprint for success!"
—*Sean Ammirati, author of* The Science of Growth

"To get ahead, above all else, respect yourself and your talents. *Hustle* is a manifesto for doing just that."
—*Jordan Harbinger, host of* The Art of Charm

"We live in a time more rife with possibility than any preceding point in history. The difference between those that take advantage and those that remain in the Cycle of Suck? Hustle. Inspiring, educational, and fun, *Hustle* is essential reading for anyone looking to do work that matters."
—*Taylor Pearson, author of* The End of Jobs

HUSTLE

THE **POWER** TO **CHARGE** YOUR LIFE WITH **MONEY,** **MEANING, AND** **MOMENTUM**

NEIL PATEL
PATRICK VLASKOVITS
JONAS KOFFLER

RODALE.

RODALE *wellness*

Live happy. Be healthy. Get inspired.

Sign up today to get exclusive access to our authors, exclusive bonuses, and the most authoritative, useful, and cutting-edge information on health, wellness, fitness, and living your life to the fullest.

Visit us online at RodaleWellness.com
Join us at RodaleWellness.com/Join

Copyright © 2016 by Neil Patel, Patrick Vlaskovits, and Jonas Koffler

All rights reserved.
Published in the United States by Rodale Books, an imprint of Random House, a division of Penguin Random House LLC, New York.
rodalebooks.com

RODALE and the Plant colophon are registered trademarks of Penguin Random House LLC.

Library of Congress Cataloging-in-Publication Data is available upon request.

ISBN 978-0-593-13716-1
Ebook ISBN 978-1-62336-717-6

Printed in the United States of America

Book design by Joanna Williams

10 9 8 7 6 5 4 3 2

We inspire health, healing, happiness, and love in the world.
Starting with you.

WELL, WELL. WE'VE FOUND YOU.

Trust us, it wasn't by luck or coincidence, though we believe in both.

Our *Hustle* book did what we had intended for it.

It grabbed you, pulled you in, and spoke to something inside of you.

Now it's your turn.

There's something left unfinished. Something big.

The sooner you get through this book, the sooner you can get started.

CONTENTS

PART THREE: HABITS

PREFACE

"To be honest, I don't believe you."

It was the fall of 2012, and Neil had just come off a conference stage to rousing applause after delivering the keynote on the latest trends in digital marketing to 2,500 enthused marketers. He'd ended his talk encouraging his audience to embrace entrepreneurial "hustle" as paramount to success and had been feeling good about his performance.

Startled, he turned to face his accuser, a petite dark-haired woman, and asked, "Excuse me?"

"C'mon on, Neil," she replied. "You know the best way to be successful is to be born to rich parents. Look around you, all the winners come from privileged backgrounds."

Shaking his head, Neil responded, "Well, with my first job I had the *privilege* of mopping up bathrooms at the amusement park near our home. I'm living proof that hustle works."

His voice faded as he saw his answer obliterated by his accuser's seething disbelief. She rolled her eyes and jabbed the air between them with the pen she had been using to take notes.

"It's rigged. Look at Bill Gates. Mark Zuckerberg. Chelsea Clinton. If you didn't go to Harvard or Stanford, you're locked out of the club. No club, no connections. No connections, no opportunities. No opportunities, no chance at real success."

Unwilling to wait for further explanation from the former theme park bathroom attendant turned Internet marketing icon and start-up founder, the dark-haired woman stormed past Neil down the long convention center hall.

Irritation at his inability to convince his accuser trailed Neil the whole evening as he navigated the conference after-party, his frustration snapping at him like an overzealous border collie amid back-slapping beer-breathed colleagues, overly loud music, and unlimited free cocktails.

As much as he tried to shake it, he knew he had to prove that dark-haired woman wrong.

Yet like her, there are millions of frustrated people among us: professionals and students, artists and entrepreneurs, moms and dads, to name a few. We know these people well. They're our friends, our coworkers, and our family members.

Every Sunday evening, those of us who have fallen for the normal rules of work and social convention sink into a mild depression as the Monday Blues set in. Our children, our spouses, our hobbies—life's little gifts—fade into the background as we are overwhelmed by the sheer drudgery that awaits us the next day at 8:00 a.m.

Nearly 90 percent of our fellow workers feel emotionally disconnected from their jobs, and their dreams remain far afield or fleeting memories. Were we uniquely privileged Masters of the Universe, we could easily bypass the slog that provides our daily bread and butter.

But let's be honest: Most of us aren't exactly "special."

We don't boast an Ivy League education like Sheryl Sandberg, a political pedigree like a Kennedy, or a wealthy father like Donald Trump. We're stuck behind our steering wheels each morning, bound by our commute, unable to take shortcuts like the privileged few. The best we can hope for is to occasionally take the carpool lane.

The reality is that we're more like Rocky Balboa than Luke Skywalker—the Force isn't strong in us. We have no special advantages. In fact, we face a world of disadvantages—at best, we're underdogs fighting a system that stacks the odds against us and squeezes the life out of us.

Today, what the three of us, Neil, Patrick, and Jonas, see going on around us is a small group of people doing well, and this is troubling. Some of these people are doing exceptionally well—some are even our close friends and clients, people we respect. And an ocean of others, some of them insanely talented people, are struggling to move beyond paycheck to paycheck and keep the promises they made to themselves and their families. We see too many people repressed by irrational and incessant fears, stifled by an unwillingness to take more risk, trapped by tough choices about their futures.

What's happened to *their* dreams? Why are so many good, hard-working people going nowhere so fast while so few prosper? What's the difference between the successful and the unfulfilled? Something is broken here. We want to fix it and in the process help thousands of people the world over become better dreamers and more confident doers.

So how do we possibly find a way to break free and achieve lasting success and fulfillment on our terms?

One way: We hustle.

In a world of boundless abundance, the only thing standing between us and fulfillment of our dreams is self-imposed friction, a poison that saps our willingness to step out of what feels comfortable.

This book is the antidote.

INTRODUCTION

NOT YOUR DADDY'S HUSTLE

"Good things happen to those who hustle."

—Anaïs Nin

Some months ago, when Patrick told his father that he and his coauthors were writing the book you are reading right now, his father asked in all earnestness, "Why would you write a book about stealing?"

Patrick's answer was telling: "Because we're stealing *hustle* back."

Since its inception in the human language, *hustle* has carried a distinct energy. It has meant different things to different people. In the late 1600s, the term was derived from the middle Dutch word *hutselen*, a verb meaning "to shake." Over the past few years, the word *hustle* has evolved from a dirty word meaning "to steal" or "to con" to an inspirational catchall verb meaning "to make something happen" or "to push forward in spite of the odds or obstacles in one's way."

This most recent drift in the word's meaning is not accidental, nor is it trivial. This change portends big shifts in our culture, from the way we raise our children to the way we interact with the traditional socioeconomic institutions of the world—from the corporations that employ us to the entrepreneurial forces that compel us to create new companies to the governments that regulate us and the educational system that teaches us.

But the current rate of economic and cultural change we are experiencing right now is unprecedented, and hustle demands a new definition.

We define hustle as:

> Decisive movement toward a goal, however indirect, by which the motion itself manufactures luck, surfaces hidden opportunities, and charges our lives with more money, meaning, and momentum.

Hustle's redefined meaning not only captures its essence in a useful manner but also acts as an unmistakable expression of today's zeitgeist, a strategy for benefiting from a fast-moving and uncertain world, one in which globalization and the prospect of ravenous software eating the world (and our jobs) impact our family's lives and our careers in real time.

In the face of such volatility, we seek agency, a way to exert our power and presence and find a place of permanence; we seek a way to achieve more self-direction, confidence, and a well of opportunity to sustain us.

Hustle is how we use our idiosyncrasies to find our unique means and our own personal successes. Discovering *our own way*, not blindly aping the success of others, is the truest way forward.

Hustle is *the* most important tool of the New American Dream, in which we reassert power and control over the system by *owning our dreams*.

To fully own your dreams, you'll need three fundamental forces: money, meaning, and momentum. Your hustle aims to cultivate and amplify those three forces throughout your life, through all you do and all you are to become as a person. When done right, hustle is the proverbial gift that keeps on giving.

The need for money, for most of us, is rather obvious—cash gives us confidence, fuels our material needs, and allows us to keep score. But money without meaning creates a vacuum inside that cannot be sated, no matter how much more money we make. Meaning, the "why" of our toil and struggle—the reason we get up in the morning and face the day—needs money as much as money needs meaning. The two together, in the right proportions, give rise to momentum. And when you have momentum, you are unstoppable. It's that spring in your step, that confidence to not ask permission but simply get things done on your terms.

If like a Jedi Knight, the Forces of Hustle are already strong in you, if you are more special than most, if you can move spacecraft with the wave of a hand, if success comes far too easily, and if the world goes out of its way to fulfill your every need, then it's unlikely you'll need this book for anything other than leisure reading or laughter.

But if you're like most people, like the woman whom Neil ran into, and if you're feeling stuck or stifled, if you haven't been given a fair shake, if you aren't getting the breaks that you deserve and are ready to make your own lucky breaks happen, if you're a "dreamer" ready to become a "doer," if you feel like an outsider or perhaps have even lost your way or forgotten that there is another way, keep reading, friend. Because when you choose to own your dreams, you join a group of underdogs, innovators, and everyday risk takers who are tipping the balance of power and willfully reshaping the future of success on their own terms.

We call these people the Hustle Generation. Welcome to our club.

Why Us?

Years before he became a successful entrepreneur and Internet icon, Neil Patel crossed the pond from London, England, to southern California. As first-generation immigrants, his family settled on the West Coast to pursue the dream of greater freedom and economic mobility. Neil's parents slowly pushed their way into the middle class, doing whatever it took to advance. His mother taught school for free until she found a full-time job; his father worked in a variety of businesses. In keeping with the immigrant's ethic of grinding it out, Neil learned to prosper by working his tail off, taking risks, and keeping an open mind for opportunities that could reward him handsomely.

Life wasn't without its challenges. For a spell, Neil worked as a restroom attendant at Knott's Berry Farm theme park, a job that taught him about humility, responsibility, and the power of air fresheners. Later, he traded up and became a door-to-door vacuum salesman, trying to convince harried customers to drop $1,600 on futuristic dust collectors. Eventually, after failing to sell a single unit, he discovered his talent for online marketing and launched his consulting business. By the time he was 21 years old, the *Wall Street Journal* had named him one of the top influencers on the Web and he was making tens of thousands of dollars a month.

And then his dream collapsed. He found himself a million dollars in debt due to a start-up effort gone horribly awry. He had paid two people to run the company—even bought them a house—and they'd run off with his investment. Awful? Yes. But that's when Neil's real hustle kicked in. Less than a year later, he had paid the million dollars off, largely by selling consulting services around his marketing expertise, doing speaking engagements, and fearlessly going after deals. He has helped dozens of Fortune 500 companies grow their online traffic and profitability. And he has become an unquestionable big deal as *the* leading online marketer in the world.

Today, Neil teaches others about Internet marketing at Quicksprout .com, his top-ranked blog, which provides no-nonsense entrepreneurship advice to millions of readers every year.

Like Neil, Patrick Vlaskovits knows the mentality and hurdles that come from being part of an immigrant family. Seeking their American Dream, Patrick's parents moved the family from Europe to hypercompetitive Silicon Valley in northern California when he was 6 years old. Broken English, strange lunch boxes, and "samer" unstylish clothing were the norms of his childhood. Patrick spoke only German and Hungarian until learning English in the first grade.

With his blue eyes and blond hair, he might have resembled his neighbors, but Patrick wasn't raised like a stereotypical Californian. Instead, his home life was regimented, defined by austerity, scarcity, and the acrimonious divorce of his parents.

To escape, Patrick created a playground of the mind. He ceaselessly devoured books, causing his third-grade teacher to remark, "I wish he'd stop reading during class and listen to me instead." He also developed a lifelong love for acquiring knowledge and adventure. Patrick committed to owning a dream different than his parents'—and he has done just that.

Patrick, whose parents and teachers thought he was destined to be a perpetual underachiever, has authored a *New York Times* bestseller, founded start-ups, and built a business advising innovative entrepreneurs and Fortune 500 companies around the world.

Jonas Koffler was raised by unconventional parents—professional nomads with a passion for ideas and a contempt for authority; in other words, Jewish academics. And while not an immigrant himself, Jonas felt like one as he moved around to more than a dozen states and several countries, developing greater resilience with each move, learning a lot about people, places, and the power of working independently to solve his own problems. As a teenager, he found a loving, stable home with his eccentric, human rights activist French aunt and his uncle, a painter, union negotiator, and his wrestling coach. They became his guardians, tribal elders who taught him more about the art of living and hustling than anyone else.

While working at a start-up in his twenties, Jonas suffered a massive stroke, rendering him temporarily blind and unable to communicate. He lost access to his memory and some motor skills and was misdiagnosed with multiple sclerosis. He overcame these stumbling blocks and worked his way back to full health through yoga and meditation. In the process, he learned to let go of fear, question reality, and build a life around stimulating pursuits that enabled him to develop his talents. He launched a creative media consultancy and achieved results he had always dreamed of.

Neil, Patrick, and Jonas have each gained a level of influence, respect, trust, and security that has provided the opportunity to hatch multimillion-dollar ventures on the backs of napkins; the freedom to travel and work anywhere; the ability to hobnob with the brilliant, rich, and famous; and the power to transform the world into a better place. These are privileges they never would have enjoyed had they continued to rent their dreams.

These are privileges you can have, too. If we've learned anything, it's that you don't have to be privileged to hustle. You only need to give yourself permission. The rest, i.e., money, meaning, and momentum, will take care of itself.

———————

Visit **HustleGeneration.com** for free tools, resources, and more.

OVERVIEW

The Broad Strokes

By the time you get through reading *Hustle,* you'll be ready to get the "more" you deserve, transform your life, and take ownership of your dreams and destiny. To help you do just that, we've divided *Hustle* into three parts: Heart, Head, and Habits.

We open Part One: Heart, by taking a hard look at the rigged system so many of us are operating in. Everywhere we look, society's landlords thwart us and trap us into a falsely limited menu of options for the way we live, work, and play. In short, they rent us our dreams. When we are defined by others' terms and limitations, we become trapped in a pattern of deferral and delay, putting off our own economic and emotional fulfillment.

In this section, we also look at how powerful social and economic forces like debt can exacerbate the effects of our limitations. Yet hearteningly, it is totally possible to change the trajectory of our lives. This process requires only subtle tweaks to our lifestyles, not seismic shifts.

Next, we examine a troubling phenomenon that might seem familiar: There's a nagging, intangible "more" that we seek in our lives, yet it remains desperately elusive. We've named this the Mediocrity of Meh. We explore why we feel this "meh" and how we've arrived at a place of learned helplessness. When we choose to avoid failure over pursuing success, we develop an unhealthy penchant for risk aversion. We've been sabotaging ourselves without really knowing it by taking on hidden risks. It doesn't have to be this way: We'll show you how to take more of the right type of risk in your life.

Take stock of how you feel about your life and ask yourself, Am I moving—at times even frantically—but getting nowhere? If so, you are probably stuck in a dangerous and habitual Cycle of Suck. You're not technically depressed, but you're not exactly happy, either. You are not alone! Many of us feel it, too, and feel equally helpless to escape it. We know there is more out there, but we just shrug our shoulders and don't care anymore. Fortunately, Cycles of Suck can be reversed, and *Hustle* will show you how to do that.

The first step is to find the heart of your true talents by taking the time and effort to allow them to come to the surface. Despite our best intentions, our talents often remain buried and elusive, hidden underneath the shoulds, maybes, and wishes of our rented dreams. The best thing we can do to remedy this tragic waste of potential is to expose ourselves to challenging projects and environments in our work and life and to focus on the unexpected strengths that *will* rise to the surface when we do so.

We've been taught that a path of 10,000 committed hours is the best and only way to master a skill. But those who hustle successfully know there's a better alternative than striving for the false goal of mastery. Instead of burying our untested talents by conforming to the plans of others, we discover that we, ourselves, must figure out what our genuine talents and abilities are. We do this by short-circuiting the Lake Wobegon effect—and forcing our talents to the surface.

We close Part One by reminding readers that they aren't insects, specialized for one role for their entire lives. Instead, they should endeavor to be flexible generalists who intelligently avoid the Perils of Perfection and free themselves to move from what is to what could be.

In Part Two: Head, we examine the strategies that can pull us out of the Cycles of Suck and help us clear our own best paths to owning our dreams. We introduce the concept of "hormesis," the observation that repeated exposure to small doses of stressors *strengthens* us. We need small amounts of pain to make the gains that prevent our existing skills from atrophying. In small doses, stress helps us grow our future skills and knowledge and helps us anticipate and solve complex challenges.

Once you have accepted that small amounts of pain are the greatest agents for growth, you can begin to think about your future more boldly. Have a great but somewhat risky idea that has terrific potential but isn't a 100 percent sure thing? It turns out, it's not the number of hits or home runs we get that matters; we can instead manifest our success by simply stepping up to the plate more often. In doing so, we can manufacture four distinct types of luck: Random Luck, Hustle Luck, Hidden Luck, and Quirky Luck. At the intersection of hustle and luck, a universal truth emerges: Choosing to own our dreams doesn't teach us how to be lucky but rather how to run out of "unluck."

As we move along our journey, there will of course be bumps along the way. Sometimes we will fail and need to regroup. Sometimes a plan will have unintended outcomes that you need to step back and make sense of. Rarely does our trip in life move directly from point A to point B. Instead we find a path that stops and starts, lurches sideways and even backward as we attempt to move forward. So why try to pretend that the best path to success is a straight line? This is where we introduce the concept of "obliquity": the indirect nature of hustle that makes each individual journey of money, meaning, and momentum unique and significant.

The reason hustle and obliquity are so well matched is that while hustle has you finding your own gifts, obliquity has you putting them to use in unique ways.

As you progress on your hustle journey, you'll discover the Three Unseen Laws of Hustle: (1) Do Something That Moves You; (2) Keep Your Head Up and Your Eyes Open; and (3) Seal the Deal and Make It Real.

Finally, we will show that doing the wrong thing (falling in love with the wrong type of person, taking a job for the wrong reasons, trying to become someone you are incapable of becoming) is often a necessary step toward finding that right thing.

In Part Three: Habits, we will reveal the exciting upside potential that smart hustlers share with nimble companies who set themselves up for explosive growth through successful initial public offerings.

We see that people, like companies, can pop—by breaking out and rapidly increasing their value in the market—and that individuals, whether managers, entrepreneurs, or artists, should develop a Personal Opportunity Portfolio (POP). A POP is the guiding plan for organizing and making sense of all our hustle efforts, and we have provided you with the tools you need to put together a POP that will help you sail forward in your own hustling. We will also unlock the power of the 10-Minute Rule, which just might change your approach to work and life entirely.

Although you may not know it, you've been assembling parts of your POP throughout your life. Now, with our help, it's time for you to determine how those parts fit into the four key categories: Potential (how we develop greater capabilities), People (how we cultivate community), Projects (how we express creativity), and Proof (how we capture credibility).

It doesn't matter if you're starting out in the workforce, making a leap to a new career, starting a small company, selling your art, or growing a much bigger and more established venture, the game of POP is fluid. Anyone can play at any time in life or work—so wherever you find yourself, developing your POP is the way forward.

There are multiple approaches to getting ahead and moving forward in your work or career plan, and all of them will be enhanced once you have learned how to hustle. We'll also show you a specific set of predictable movements, which we call the Fourfold Path. From Outside/Inside Hustle (the foot in the door), Inside/Upside Hustle (promotion should you choose to ascend the corporate ladder), Inside/Outside Hustle (movement from one organization to another or toward entrepreneurial pastures), to Outside/Upside Hustle (the explosive or sustained entrepreneurial growth model), you'll be able to choose the adventure that best suits your situation.

Our goal in writing this book has been to show how the right mix of momentum and money can lead us toward meaning. The three Ms organically align and combine to enrich our lives as we find the energy to sustain an infinite hustle.

If you've made it this far, you're ready to step up to the plate. The game begins . . .

"I am not what happened to me . . .
I am what I choose to become."

—Carl Gustav Jung

PART ONE
HEART

"One sees clearly only with the heart.
Anything essential is invisible to the eyes."
—THE FOX IN *THE LITTLE PRINCE* BY ANTOINE DE SAINT-EXUPÉRY

I

DON'T RENT YOUR DREAMS, OWN THEM

"There's a simple doctrine. Outside of a person's love, the most sacred thing that they can give is their labor. And somehow or another along the way, we tend to forget that. And labor is a very precious thing that you have. And any time that you can combine labor with love, you've made a merger."
—James Carville in *The War Room*

Not Simply a Means to an End

The work we choose to do reflects who we are. It's not intended to be some trivial endeavor or accidental outlet. But we cannot escape the fact that too many of us spend our best years working harder than ever with less to show for it than ever before.

By day, we're trapped in the monotony of unfulfilling work and jobs that may well disappear tomorrow, and by night, we're buried under the mounting pressure of credit card and student loan debts. We waste years of our lives spinning around an unforgiving hamster wheel of arbitrary rules and irrational fears. We defer our freedom to an antiquated nine-to-five system controlled by others. And yet we see some people control their destinies, own their dreams, and reap their riches—and, in some small way, change the world for the better. They've figured out something many of us have overlooked.

In the 20th century, we all trusted a rewards system that seemed to work. As we pursued the middle-class dream of mobility, we put our noses to the grindstone and toiled. We accepted the rules and in return we enjoyed a fair salary, job security, affordable housing, and lives better than the ones our parents had. These days, however, loyalty doesn't translate into success, and "leaning in" doesn't lead to fulfillment. As we're asked to take on increasingly greater burdens for fewer rewards, we are no longer promised the security, protection, or consistency that used to be the trade-off for chaining ourselves to the plans of others. Meanwhile, while we're denied the pursuit of authentic freedom, others seize opportunities for creative expression and discover *work they enjoy* in settings supportive of their talents and, in turn, find the life they want. Their ends, their dreams, justify the means. Yours can too.

So What Happened to Our Dreams?

> **ACHTUNG BABY:** The next couple of pages could sting, and that is by design. Put on your big boy pants and keep reading as we make sense of how we got here.

Once upon a time, in a society much like this one, nearly anyone with a decent work ethic and a desire to grow could build a solid career with stability and upward mobility. This was a time when that little house with the white picket fence was within the reach of every man and woman. Yet in our jobless economy, we are pounded by the forces of globalization, the inflation they say "doesn't exist" diminishes any salary gains, most of us are wage slaves living check to check and month to month, and few of us have saved much for the hard times that will come.

In the United States today, 40 million of us are chained to onerous student loans that clip our wings, and more than 20 million of us are confined to our parents' nests. We ask ourselves, What happened to an education that cost less than a house? Anyone? Bueller? Bueller?

Speaking of homes, how about owning a home you can afford to keep? Oh, the irony of buying a house these days! On your way to the poorhouse, so many of us become "house poor" first. Around the globe, millions echo our experience, working hard yet feeling stifled by a stew of uncertainty, becoming less sure about their futures by the day.

Dear Millennials and Gen Xers:
It wasn't always like this.
We're truly sorry.
Signed:

THE BABY BOOMERS AND
THE GREATEST GENERATION

It's a troubling state of affairs. Just as we start to make more money, when we finally feel as if we're getting ahead, the tax system slaps us back to reality. What happened to our own piece of the dream and the freedom to live our lives under rules that make sense?

Is the American Dream alive or dead? That depends on whom you ask. A 2015 survey from the Institute of Politics at Harvard University asked 18- to 29-year-olds that very question. Respondents were nearly evenly split: 48 percent answered "Dead" and 49 percent favored the affirmative "Alive." Interestingly, nearly 58 percent of college graduates said the dream was alive for them personally, whereas only 42 percent of noncollege graduates felt the same way.[1]

Among our 30- and 40-something peers, whom we informally polled, the results were about the same, with nearly half believing the American Dream to be either dead or in purgatory. This got us thinking that perhaps some of the political rhetoric of late is right. Maybe there's a bigger game in play? One we're aware of but can't clearly see.

Yes, Virginia, the Game *Is* Rigged

If you've ever felt as if you were a pawn in someone else's chess match, you're in good company. Legendary comedian George Carlin captured it wryly when he said, "It's a big club, and you ain't in it . . . They tell you what to believe, what to think, what to buy. The table is tilted folks, the game is rigged and nobody seems to notice, nobody seems to care."

Whether you choose to accept Carlin's disheartening outlook or dismiss it, reality reflects that everyone is playing the same game of success among unseen spiderwebs. And the game of success is one of complacency and conformity.

Here's a little secret: We're not playing that game. You shouldn't either.

The age-old tropes for how to live are just models for complacency and conformity: Sit at your school desk, do your work, get good grades, get a car, get hitched, string together some decent jobs, purchase a home and have 2.2 kids, and in 40 years you can retire, idle, and die. Gotcha!

Place our trust in today's system? Please. It's a rigged game designed to snare us from the onset of our adult lives with student loans, credit cards, bloated mortgages, unfulfilling work that quickly gets outsourced to the lowest bidder, overpriced health care, and quickly commoditized McJobs. And the majority who run with the herd hate their jobs anyway. It's no exaggeration. According to research from the Gallup organization, where, incidentally, Jonas once worked— and hated his job—nearly 90 percent of workers around the world feel emotionally disconnected from what they do professionally. Their jobs are more often a source of frustration than one of fulfillment.

The most maddening aspect of this conundrum is that by following all the old rules, we ourselves hold the hand that holds us down. That is, the system seems hell-bent on keeping us in line, and even if we have thousands of reasons to hit the eject button and figure out a better way, we always seem to find an excuse to justify staying stuck.

And as we well know, it sucks.

Not on Sale This Week: The American Dream

Conventional thinking dictates that college is paramount to cultivating a mind capable of critical thought, which leads us down the path toward a meaningful career. On second thought, it is clear that the ability to think critically does, indeed, lead us down that path. But college may or may not be a part of that story. Of course, the college experience may offer value other than mere edification, but any way you look at it, that edification is not exactly inexpensive these days, with the average cost of a 4-year degree in the United States rising dangerously above six figures, two to three times as expensive as colleges in Canada[2] and astronomically pricey when compared to no-cost universities in Germany, where fearless Americans and other foreign students have begun to flock to enjoy obvious advantages. But for those who opt to stay within our borders for their education, have no fear: You can always just take out a loan.

And we have. Oh, we have.

The collective amount of student debt owed in the United States has jumped in recent years. Outstanding student loans totaled $516 billion in 2007. By late 2015, student loans had more than doubled, to $1.2 trillion ($1,200,000,000,000)—with 12, count 'em 12, digits after the 1. That's an unprecedented 130 percent increase in about 8 years. To make matters worse, real wages for recent graduates have fallen. The national average salary for those who get jobs sits at around $45,000. But the average college graduate holds more than $30,000 in student debt upon graduation. If a student goes on to graduate school, that debt is likely to balloon to six figures.

What happens when you cannot find a job but still need to make student loan payments to pay for that overpriced degree? You're out of luck, and now you're neck-deep in credit card debt as well.

Unlike credit card debt, student loan debt is virtually impossible to discharge through the existing legal bankruptcy procedures. That's a bit odd, isn't it?

Remember, for consumers, bankruptcy is a way to protect us from being indebted for the rest of our lives by our own poor decision making or unfortunate circumstances. People young and old can legally petition the courts to do away with all types of debt, even those acquired through greed and poor judgment. Idiotic debts incurred

through the purchase of luxury goods like that Nautique wake boat
we couldn't afford, poorly thought-out loan guarantees, unpaid taxes,
et cetera, can all be discharged through bankruptcy proceedings. And
yet, student loans remain near immune to such consideration.

Bankruptcy courts are more likely to discharge a foolish gambling
debt than a student debt made in good faith. Does that make any
sense? It does, but only in a rigged system designed to benefit, guess
who? The people whose investment portfolios own our debt in the
form of collateralized student loan asset-backed securities (SLABs).
That's our system, like it or not.

Today's graduates find themselves trapped in a system that forces
them to pay down higher student debts with lower wages, making it
all the more likely they'll have no choice but to rent, not own, their
dreams in a desperate attempt to keep their heads above the waters of
rising debt. That means taking meaningless jobs. Anthropologist
David Graeber, author of *Debt: The First 5,000 Years*, summed it up
best: If there's a way of a society committing mass suicide, what better
way than to take all the youngest, most energetic, creative, joyous
people in your society and saddle them with, like, $50,000 of debt so
they have to be slaves? There goes your music. There goes your culture. There goes everything new that would pop out. And in a way,
this is what's happened to our society. We're a society that has lost any
ability to incorporate the interesting, creative, and eccentric people.

In case you're curious, savvy employers can exploit the debt dis-
advantage of younger workers, knowing that new law school graduates, for example, hold an average of more than $84,000 in student
loans. Law firms enjoy incredible leverage in determining salaries and
working hours. After all, when you need to start making student loan
payments, you need a job. And to keep that job, you'd better keep your
nose clean, kid.

Debt and its discontents are not merely an American phenomenon. Instead, debt's a universal reality, which by design hands us a
double-edged sword. On the one hand, loans provide us access to
education and a much-needed lifeline to finance us through our rough

times and keep our budgets and businesses afloat, those of your authors included. On the other hand, if mismanaged or misunderstood, debt can become an insidious instrument with crushing consequences. So borrower beware: Tread lightly and be grateful if your bet on debt works out.

It is worth nothing that our Australian brethren have a household debt—including mortgages, credit cards, and personal loans—that rises above that of any other country, at more than 130 percent of GDP.[3] Paradoxically, our friends down under are some of the happiest people in the world.

Our lack of money often forces us into making life-changing considerations that can't be taken lightly. There are forces other than money, such as our love for our families and desire for freedom, that force us to shake ourselves free of unfulfilling routine and search for opportunities.

Say Hello to My Little Friend: Freedom

In present-day Cuba, loans are basically nonexistent, and the same goes for free enterprise. The institutionalized lack of consumer choice, near-zero opportunity for social mobility, and absence of rewards from a labor system organized by the overlords of an antiquated, underfunded socialist system drive much frustration and misery.

The societal changes under way remain slow going, but an undercurrent of optimism and disruption runs through the streets, palpable to all, signaling a dramatic transformation in the not-too-distant future. Jonas and his wife, Laura, were excited to experience this firsthand during a recent visit, as they took a closer look at the emerging dreamers and doers, those hustling to drive change in the economy and make a life on their own terms.

"Treinta dólares."

Gliding along the Malecón en route to Old Havana, their driver, let's call him Ernesto, recounted his story. "I trained as an electrical engineer at the top school in Cuba. The equivalent of a master's degree in the United States," said Ernesto. "And for my education, you know what I receive? Thirty dollars a month from the government."

Ernesto and his wife, Luci, a nurse, are the proud parents of two young children. Together, they earned about $40 a month, barely enough to buy milk, meat, soap, clothes, and other staples not provided in their rations, a monthly guarantee of certain consumer goods granted to all Cubans by the government.

Ernesto had long dreamed of running his own business designing energy-efficient electrical systems. But operating a private business is really an exercise in futility when government bureaucrats dictate your every move and siphon away any and every dollar you might make.

A few years into the couple's marriage, Ernesto faced a critical choice: He could operate within the rules—in other words, show up to his job, be a loyal supporter of the Cuban revolution, and keep quiet—or he could bend the rules and follow his dream of operating a private business. The latter choice would have to come outside the purview of the Cuban government, and it would come at the risk of a 10-year prison sentence if he were caught. Stay the course or challenge the accepted system to provide exponentially more money, meaning, and momentum for his family.

Extreme risk flies in the face of logic. It leads to profound existential questions such as: What lies on the other side—prison or plunder? How much of a sacrifice am I willing to take on to care for my family? Faced by the same conundrum, what might you do? Accept and abide by the limitations of a corrupt system or find a way to push your own dreams forward and create more freedom in spite of the risk?

Ernesto opted for door number two. Staying the course and working within the confines of the system was no longer a choice, not if he wanted freedom and meaningful options for his family. He started improvising, confidently planning how to create deals to work with the foreigners he knew, liked, and felt he could confide in. He would offer his underappreciated, undervalued, and unlicensed engineering skills and work by building, renovating, and wiring electrical systems, designing spaces, translating, and being an on-the-ground fixer as needed.

He made a list: There were the Brazilian businessmen, Paolo and Luca, for whom he had done translation several months back. And that French diplomat, Claude, who had expressed interest in renovating a small hotel in an international neighborhood on the outskirts of Havana. There were others, too, like groups of Americans who wanted private tours. When he looked for it, Ernesto found himself basking in the opportunity to make more money than ever.

And thus, Ernesto accelerated his success. He built a head of steam by landing his first gig wiring an office for the Brazilians. He proved his worth by sourcing virtually impossible to find parts and wiring equipment by bartering milk and car parts. As he made more money, he put together a team of a few trustworthy people who, like him, wanted a leg up. And as a group, they renovated a decrepit building nearing collapse on the edges of suburban Havana, turning it into a sparkling boutique hotel. They built camaraderie. And they kept their lips sealed.

Although he had struck gold, a newfound stress weighed on Ernesto. He started to wonder if anyone around him could be an informant. Would Camilo, his unbearable in-law upstairs, rat him out? Or would the functionaries doing the inspection rounds on the renovation site begin to ask questions? And then there was the threat of an accidental slipup by the clients paying him under the table, de rigueur in Cuba's informal work sector. One can only imagine the kind of toll that took on his psyche (not to mention his hairline). And still he persevered.

Ernesto's ultimate goal was to set himself and his family free. And if that meant some bending of the rules and well-planned diversionary tactics, it was worth it.

The day Ernesto stepped away from his unlicensed contracting business, he, Luci, and their kids stepped into a *costal de dinero* (sack of cash) 100 times greater than the $40 a month they'd previously lived on.

They stashed away enough money—literally placed it in a hole in their garden—so that they could afford to buy milk, meat, and other staples. Eventually they had enough to invest in an old Chevy convertible, for which they paid the unfathomable sum of $11,000—in cash! Keep in mind, most Cubans make around $300 per year. And now, that 1954 Bel Air serves as a taxi, and Ernesto's likely still hustling at this very moment, gliding down the Avenida Paseo toward Plaza de la Revolución and untold destinations, wearing a proud smile on his face and knowing he chose wisely to reject the rules and change the game to own his dreams.

Even amid the most extreme situations, when we're overcome by fear and self-doubt, we must pursue an upside path. When not under dire Communism or threat of life in prison, the Hustle Generation discovers power in doing. We must trust that the reward is worth the risk and find the courage to put ourselves in motion. We owe it to ourselves to steal back control of our lives from a broken system. We must make choices that enable us to move freely and forcefully forward. We must move toward our dreams, and as we chase better outcomes, we get to choose our own adventure. In a word, we must hustle.

Owning Your Dreams Gives You Unlimited Upside

We live at a time when more people are buying and owning more stuff than at any other time in history. We own more cars and more smartphones; we own bitcoins; we have more bling, more clothes than we can ever wear, more plastic toys than our children can even imagine the time to play with, and more immaterial material possessions than we can conceive of.

Unlike the mountains of forlorn toys in many homes across America (certainly in Patrick's home), which depreciate and eventually end up in a trash heap or junkyard, dreams can only appreciate in value. They feed our soul. They give us direction. We may fill our days playing the short game by collecting material things. Yet owning our dreams is the ultimate long game. So it's absurd that we'd prioritize owning the hottest new device, cool car, or trendy toy over owning that which makes us feel most engaged and most alive.

Is the dream you're racing toward something you can own? It will be if you choose to make it so. That dream need not be terribly complicated. It's a personal, subjective dream you aspire to. For Ernesto, the dream was about self-respect, choice, and mobility, and about being able to provide for his family at a higher income level than his government allowed. Maybe for you it's something like waking up in the morning to do the kind of work that makes you feel alive, a calling you *must* do. Maybe it's simply having the ability to work remotely and choose working hours that align with your natural schedule. Maybe it's being able to publish a book or create your own clothing line or start a new career in a field you've always been curious about. Maybe it's making *and* giving away more money than Bill and Melinda Gates to causes like health care, hunger relief, childhood education, or whatever you care deeply about. Maybe you're not racing toward a dream at all right now, and that's something that we are here to help you change.

Choose for Yourself or Others Will Choose for You

While far from a universal reality the world over, free will and choice are basic principles of the American Dream. Every day, millions of us wake up and decide between McDonald's or Dunkin' Donuts, *The Real Housewives of* Wherever or *Keeping Up with the Kardashians*. These "choices" provide us with the illusion of free will, the sense that we have a modicum of control over our lives. But these are bread-and-circus distractions. They satiate our need for immediate comfort, but they're banal in the bigger scheme of things; at best, they're temporary distractions from the real goal of owning our dreams.

When it comes to the big choices in life, the *really BIG* ones—a career we find stifling or one that's fulfilling, a relationship we find suffocating or one that allows us to grow—too many of us choose not to choose. We delay or we opt for the path of least resistance; we go for whatever is easiest or select the choice that *appears* safe and certain. In return, we end up "renting" our dreams.

Renting our dreams means taking our current set of choices as givens, playing within the system, and never stopping to think about what might be genuinely best for ourselves. Because listening to the little voice inside you, the one that whispers to you about the "more" that's out there for you to grasp, will only lead to trouble and turmoil. No, no, no—you'd best stay on the beaten path and accept that your life is fine the way it is. But how good could our lives be when we've never stopped to think about what would bring us the most fulfillment?

Owning your dreams feels different, perhaps even strange. It involves living an engaged life; making your best, most decisive choices; not being afraid of the consequences; and correcting your course along the way. It means taking action and assuming rightful ownership of your destiny.

Renting our dreams manifests in being told that we should be grateful for the pittance of a salary we earn because we wouldn't get hired anywhere else "given the state of today's economy." Or when a recruiter knowingly misleads us by trying to talk us into interviewing for an entry-level position we are clearly overqualified for at a "great company with room to grow."

We rent our dreams when we accept the falsely limited menu of options provided by society's landlords for the ways we live, work, and play. You can recognize one of these landlords when you feel forced to choose from an incomplete and false set of options. No matter your choice, you lose and they win. They win because they have sold you on a conventional path where they profit from your tacit acceptance of the choices at hand.

It's as if we are shopping for a home and have walked into a showroom and are told that everyone can choose *only* from among three floor plans. Sure, all three come comfortably furnished and move-in ready with a variety of color schemes, but as renters, we aren't allowed to decorate, let alone renovate to fit our specific needs and identities. The rented dream ends up dictating how we live, how we think, and how we see the world. We are defined by someone else's terms and limitations, and it is often to our detriment.

Every moment you don't make a stand against the landlords of society, you're losing ground. Every day you buy into the system, the hole you're in gets that much deeper and you get that much further away from really owning your dream. Just like the interest on your credit cards, spiritual interest compounds daily.

You should be striving constantly to find your dream home. There *are* other blueprints out there—and you can make them your own. Unlike a rental, you'll take a deeper level of responsibility and build equity instead of building equity for your landlord.

Keep in mind the *ownership* piece means that you, and specifically you, exert broader control over your daily choices in life. You do not allow yourself to be controlled by a heavy-handed spouse or a boss, parent, or teacher who dictates what you can and cannot do. A rented dream, on the other hand, places the power of choice and control—financially, emotionally, and otherwise—in the hands of someone other than you. It's a disheartening place.

When you own your dream, you build it custom to your personality and needs. Now, your home—your dream—can grow and *evolve just as you do*.

Hustle for *Your* Dreams

It's not enough to simply have a dream, you have to actively pursue it. Most people who talk endlessly about dreams but don't do anything about them are effectively choosing not to choose, and they end up with a life they don't recognize. They wonder why they feel so beaten down and defeated, but deep down they know they have another choice.

The truth is, over the long term you have only one good option: Own your dreams. If you refuse to, you become a tenant in someone else's dream. Their dream becomes your reality. How does that feel? And just imagine what your boss, Bill Lumbergh, is dreaming about (*Mmmmmmm . . . yeah*) as he takes your red stapler and dismisses you to the basement again.*

Some might ask if it's possible to both rent *and* own at the same time. No. You're either an owner or a renter. Renting might be necessary, but it must be temporary. If you're renting dreams, you're not building any dream equity of your own. So you must create an exit strategy that involves more opportunities to own your own dreams. And that's precisely why you're reading this book.

OD'ing on Dreams

Years before she transformed herself into the famed "Queen of Prime Time" (and long before everyone from your sister to your cat fell head over heels in love with dork turned McDreamy Patrick Dempsey), Shonda Rhimes, the creator of the television series *Grey's Anatomy* and *Scandal,* found that dreams didn't push her forward but instead held her back.

Rhimes recounted this during a commencement address at Dartmouth College. "I blue sky'ed it like crazy," she recalled. "I dreamed and dreamed. And while I was dreaming, I was living in my sister's basement. Dreamers often end up living in the basements of relatives, FYI."

Too much dreaming leads to too little doing. With daydreams, night dreams, dream boards, dream catchers, dream jobs, dream dates, we reach a catatonic state of overdreaming. We dream so much that we never move an inch from optimistic thought into full-motion fruition.

Anyone, even our best friend, Simon the dog, can dream.

That's not the problem.

Rhimes argued that it's the doing, not the dreaming, that gets you

---

* If you haven't seen Mike Judge's movie *Office Space,* be sure to add it to your list. And while you're at it, watch *Idiocracy* as well.

to a place of fulfillment. "Ditch the dream and be a doer, not a dreamer. Maybe you know exactly what it is you dream of being, or maybe you're paralyzed because you have no idea what your passion is. The truth is, it doesn't matter. You don't have to know. You just have to keep moving forward."

That's sage advice, and just as important, know that owning your dream means going beyond just mere dreaming. In case you're confused, here's a simple rule to remember: *Dream* as a noun, great. *Dream* as a verb, not so great.

Owning your dream is the goal. Dreaming isn't.

Life's treasure map, the unknown opportunities ahead, can only take solid form once we move from OD'ing (overdreaming) to DO (dream ownership). This happens when we consciously commit to moving from overdosing on our dreams to executing them. It is then when our dreams are realized. This subtle yet profound distinction leads us back to the one acceptable conclusion, the one choice that matters most: *We must hustle.*

Nobody tells you this. The secret to getting ahead is based on manageable tweaks, not tectonic shifts. Neither blue nor red pill is required. And the best part is that you get to choose your own adventure. It starts as soon as you want it to, and provided that you're still alive as you're reading this book, it's never too late to begin anew.

If you're ready to begin anew, visit HustleGeneration.com for free tools, resources, and more.

2

REPAIR THE MEH IN YOUR HEART

"Mechanization best serves the mediocre."
—Frank Lloyd Wright

How do we go about owning our dreams when every morning we set off on a long workday wishing for the best and instead find ourselves going through the meh-motions of routine sameness? We get up, we shower, we dress, and we kiss our loved ones goodbye. Lining up at the coffee shop, we seek comfort in our chai lattes. At the gym, we heft weights, hit the treadmill, and push our bodies to extremes just to feel alive. We file into yoga class and breathe deeply to reconnect with our higher selves for, say, 52 minutes a week. Yet we cannot escape feeling dissatisfied. As the esteemed social critic Louis CK observed, "Everything's amazing and nobody's happy."

That nagging, intangible "more" we seek in our lives remains elusive. We sense we should be spending time on endeavors close to our hearts, but we don't even have the words to articulate the source of our lack of fulfillment, the holes in our hearts, even to ourselves, let alone to others. Why do we feel so stifled?

Getting Fat on Zero Calories

In an effort to keep our weight in check, we keep a frosty, silver Diet Coke on our desk at work. And maybe a few in the shared office fridge as well. We look ahead to lunch when we'll wash down our pear and kale salads with that trusty, refreshing Diet Coke and lemon. Later, when out with our friends in the evening, our drink of choice is always a tall glass, tinkling with ice cubes, rum, and, you can taste it now, Diet Coke.

Mmmmmm. Delicious. Fun. And healthy! But the diet drink we've sipped so studiously all day long has been invisibly working against us, wreaking silent havoc. Its effect on our biochemistry is not helping us get skinny but, ironically, making us even fatter! Research conducted by the University of Texas Health Science Center at San Antonio suggests that over a decade, regularly imbibing our favorite sugar-free diet beverage *increases* the likelihood of an increased waist size by 70 percent.[1] And, similarly, researchers at Purdue University found that rats who took in artificial sweeteners gained *more* weight than their tailed counterparts who took in sugary foods.[2]

Worse, for us humans, especially for those of us who are mostly sedentary, and who among our office brethren and sistren aren't these days, the prospect of a spare tire or muffin top might hit close to home. As studies have shown, the more fat around our bellies, the more likely we are to develop diseases. Our lovable, huggable surface fat forcing us to loosen our belts is just the tip of a dangerous iceberg. On top of that, when we consume diet drinks, our insulin levels spike just as they would in response to sugar in normal sweet drinks, leading to roller-coaster mood swings as our bodies attempt to stabilize blood sugar levels.

We've been sabotaging ourselves without knowing it. In the mirror and in the media, we see the risks in getting fat, and in our desperation to avoid it we take on an even bigger risk. Why would we do something so, in a word, stupid? Because in the throes of our extreme risk aversion, we've locked on the wrong goal: *avoiding failure.* Our trying to *not get fat* is like avoiding failure, and it isn't the same thing as making strides toward the better option: getting fit. We can be comfortably "skinny-fat" and not be deemed fat after all, but we aren't exactly fit or healthy, though we could be with a little more effort.

Our lack of action, and the timidity that comes with the mindset of avoiding failure, invariably leads us down the path of self-sabotage, because avoiding failure is not a goal that we can actually achieve. It's an illusion. We'll never know if we have arrived, because failure could be around the corner. Avoiding failure becomes a permanent state of paranoia that leads to paralysis that dramatically increases your hidden-risk profile. When we opt only for that feel-good diet drink, we push ourselves into a dangerous trap. The better choice, as we know, would be to take care of our bodies by drinking more water and less of the delicious Diet Whatever (and, of course, coupling that with a few minutes of daily exercise). Doing so would set us in motion toward a world of upside benefits and break the routine of avoiding failure.

The way out of this conundrum is to burn into our brains that the goal is not to avoid risk and failure altogether, the goal is to achieve success by taking bite-size risks. This makes for our own success, achieved of our own means, our own direction, and our own definition. This is a success borne of our own hustle.

Wishing to Win Is Willing to Lose

In the original *Rocky* movie, Sylvester Stallone plays a journeyman boxer, Rocky Balboa, at a crossroads: He can accept the serendipitous, life-changing opportunity to put his skills on the line and fight the world champion, Apollo Creed, or remain a part-time club fighter and ruffian debt collector, a job he of course hates. Rocky's dream is to become something great: somebody, anybody other than a "bum."

To own that dream he is *willing to win*. He wants to achieve success, not avoid failure. He wants to put the pain and poverty he has endured behind him and look confidently to the training and fight ahead of him. So he trains, and when it comes time to meet Apollo Creed in the ring, he fights like he has nothing to lose and everything to gain. He leaves everything in that ring. And while he loses the fight, the trajectory of his life changes dramatically for the better.

Rocky is a fictional character. He has a dream and he owns it. In real life he doesn't exist. But you do, and in choosing to own your dreams, your opportunity looks exactly the same as Rocky's. So when you forget about avoiding failure and achieving success, what must you keep in mind?

The Weight of Hidden Risk

Imagine you have an old-time scale—the kind with two sides that have to be balanced. The object whose weight you would like to determine is placed on one side, and you incrementally add known weights to the other side until the two sides balance. You add one 500-gram weight, then two 100-gram weights, and finally a 50-gram weight. Now you know you have just bought 750 grams of the best Hungarian bacon money can buy.

Dealing with *hidden* risks is like buying that hunk of bacon and then ending up in the emergency room the next day, finding out that it had harbored a dangerous strain of salmonella. Salmonella won't register on the scale, but its presence will make you extremely ill. In our lives, we often end up eating hidden risks because we don't account for them on our internal risk scales. Failing to do so can lead to poor, sometimes tragic decisions.

In the aftermath of the horrific events of September 11, 2001, many Americans needing to travel long distances understandably opted to drive versus what they would have done before 9/11: flying the same distances. Sadly, what many of these Americans didn't account for was the hidden risk of driving long distances. It just is— statistically, and in reality—far safer to fly long distances than it is to drive them.

A 2006 Cornell University study estimated that in the 2 years following 9/11, an additional 2,302 people died from road accidents that they wouldn't have encountered had they chosen to fly. How much safer is flying than driving? By most experts' estimation, normalized per unit of distance, flying is about 65 *times safer* than driving. But it certainly doesn't *feel* that way. Every time we lift off from the runway and defy gravity, we feel like we're doing something much riskier than hopping in the car to buy a gallon of milk—even though that's just not so.

Weighing the risks, visible and invisible, for a long drive isn't as theoretical as you might have assumed. After Patrick bought a home in Austin, Texas, he had to figure out how to get his family from southern California to Texas. His first Chevy Chase-ian instinct was that a road trip would be a wonderful way to see more of the country and also allow the family a bonding trip. The thought of listening to "Holiday Road" on repeat and stopping at roadside greasy spoons every night for dinner held great appeal, but 3 days of nonstop Slug Bug and I Spy didn't seem so appealing.

But what changed his mind was the thought of driving long distances on remote roads and the nonzero possibility of being in an accident with everything that mattered to him—his family—in the car with him.

After pondering that unsettling thought, Patrick decided to avoid potentially hidden salmonella and opted to fly his family to Austin instead of drive.

We must beware of salmonella in our careers, too. We hear the statistics about how one in two small businesses fails. We see the struggle of entrepreneurs we know. We feel—deeply—the immediate loss of income when we leave our "safe" jobs. We see the skeptical look in our parents' eyes when we start a new venture rather than taking that steady-but-uninspiring job. What we don't see is the hidden risk. What are we missing? What are we giving up by remaining where we are? And what does tomorrow hold? Is that job really as steady as it seems?

In the everyday battle we fight between getting ahead and getting left behind in life and work, we find our fulfillment and freedom distinctly tied to our risk appetite. The secret is that we need to make ourselves feel hungry enough to step into the ring and break our routine of meh. The more our risk comes in bite-size, active experiences, the better. But if we're unwilling to take small risks and make the minor shifts that set us free, then we will inevitably find ourselves feeling trapped in a cycle that, much like our craving for Diet Coke, can be difficult to crack.

Cycles of Suck

Whatever your motivations, wherever you see your future, be ready to own your dreams, to commit to doing some things a bit differently, to take a meandering rather than a straight-line path, and to be open to surprises along the way. Even still, owning your dreams is tough, especially when life's washing machine has us going round and round in a "Cycle of Suck."

We start by asking ourselves, Are we moving, at times even frantically, but getting nowhere? Are we stuck in a Cycle of Suck?

Take Pete, a 34-year-old, midlevel creative director at an ad agency in Hollywood, California. Pete's Cycle of Suck might be working on uninspiring products, begetting uninspired marketing campaigns, begetting an uninspired and plodding career path, which then sees Pete working on a new uninspired brand, and the cycle starts anew.

Or Milla, a 22-year-old recent college graduate from Columbus, Ohio. Her Cycle of Suck could be getting rejected from a challenging yet interesting job because of lack of experience; biding her time by taking a McJob instead; then getting McJob work experience, not engaging her talents, and not learning. Then Milla's right back to where she started—getting turned down for yet another meaningful job because of her lack of relevant experience. Happy Meal, anyone?

Maybe you're like Max, a 49-year-old pharmaceutical executive from New Brunswick, New Jersey, passed over time and time again for a senior leadership role. Max's boss was just promoted, and his new boss sees Max as the enemy and brings in a new team. Max is ostracized and relegated to unimportant, low-status tasks. Two years later, his new boss is promoted, while Max remains shackled to the same job, same title, and same frustrations.

Or you could be just like Joyce, a 52-year-old small business owner of a leather goods retailer in Baton Rouge, Louisiana. Profits at Joyce's store were slim. The handmade purses, bags, and wallets sold adequately, but they were lower-end items. Sales performed just well enough to pay the bills and order more of the same product, which attracted the same cheap customer base so that prices stayed down and profits remained negligible.

What is terrifying about these Cycles of Suck is that through constant repetition they rewrite our expectations about our own fates and become habits. Bad habits. Bad habits are terrible for all sorts of patently obvious reasons. To pick two: Bad habits are sticky, and they become unconscious. Not only does the cycle itself become a bad habit, but we mask the suck with bread-and-circus distractions to make getting through the day less painful. We develop routines that make us feel in control but that in reality are just reinvesting in our renter's agreement.

Ever try to give up a habit, even a habit as innocuous as drinking coffee? Those of us addicted to that black brew know exactly how impossible it feels to go a morning without. "Yeah, sure. I can stop drinking coffee anytime. I just don't want to," we lie to ourselves.

But then, first thing in the morning, even before we take the time to greet our spouse, kiss our kids, or let the family dog out to do its business, we stumble bleary-eyed into the kitchen to fumble with the coffeemaker or perhaps zombie-drive to the nearest Starbucks, barely capable of speech, grunting at the barista for a venti Americano.

We don't kick the coffee habit. Because what's the harm, anyway? It is only coffee. Plus, we've been doing it for the past 20 years. Hell, having a venti Americano in the morning, and midmorning, and twice in the afternoon—it's just part of me. Did I mention it tastes great?

The coffee itself is not necessarily bad; in fact, it's a huge source of our antioxidant intake, but the addiction—our dependency on coffee—requires some rethinking. Addictions can mask other needs, like maybe we might consider other ways to generate a burst of energy or clarity in the morning.

Hustling is about shaking things up, letting go of the old patterns that suck the life out of us, and beginning anew.

Seligman's Dogs

In a well-known, shocking (literally), and ugly experiment undertaken in 1967, psychologist Martin Seligman developed an unexpected yet sublime insight critical to understanding our ability to motivate ourselves.

In his experiment, Seligman divided a group of 24 dogs into three groups of 8. The first group of dogs, the "escape group," was taught that if an electric shock was administered to them, they could terminate it by pressing their heads against panels in their enclosures.

Later, the escape group dogs were placed in a large box divided into two areas by a low barrier in the middle. When they were shocked, the dogs in the escape group yelped and jumped over the barrier to the other side that would not shock them.

The second group of dogs, the "control group," did not receive the panel-press training but were also placed in the shuttle box. When shocked, they behaved much in the same fashion, first expressing surprise and pain and then jumping the barrier in an effort to escape the shock.

With the unfortunate third group, the "yoked group," Seligman did something different. When he zapped them in their enclosures, he did so with a yoke that made the electric shocks inescapable no matter how hard or how often the poor dog pressed the panels with its head or tried to escape. Then Seligman placed the yoked group dogs into the same shuttle box that the other groups had been in. And just as before, the dogs could escape shock by simply leaping over the low barrier.

But, unlike those in the escape and control groups, the dogs in the yoked group didn't try to avoid the electric shocks, even though a possible escape route (the low barrier) was clear and present.

They had learned to be helpless.

The ultimate terrible, horrible, no good, very bad outcome of repeated trips through a Cycle of Suck isn't the suckiness. Nor is it the repetition. It's the numbing "learned helplessness," the horrific phenomenon that you might *learn to be incapable of helping yourself* in the face of life's many frictions even if a solution to your woes presents itself directly.

Just like Seligman's dogs, we've come to expect the suck. (And the suck expects us.) And when a Cycle of Suck oh-so-insidiously becomes a part of our identity, as it did for the yoked dogs who had been trained to believe that they could not escape the pain of the electric shocks, it begins to occupy our souls. When this happens, we have moved from a temporary sense of suck to a permanent suckiness.

We call this phenomenon the Mediocrity of Meh. It is a feeling of compounding, bored despair. Our senses are dulled, our expectations remain entirely deflated, our ambitions stay fast asleep, and we avoid taking action because, well, why should we?

We're not technically depressed, but we're not exactly happy, either. We know that there is a "more" out there, but we just shrug our shoulders and don't care anymore.

In some ways, the Mediocrity of Meh is worse than depression. People with depression and their families and friends know that they're depressed and can start righting their emotional ships, be it through pharmaceuticals or therapeutic treatments that help them heal. The Mediocrity of Meh tricks us into thinking that this is how it was meant to be.

We're just "meh." You're meh. I'm meh. It's a big meh world out there.

But it isn't.

There are oceans of opportunity for free expression and commerce on a global scale. Have a product idea? That same "just-in-time" global supply chain available to large enterprise is available to you, too. Nineteen-year-old millennials are starting successful businesses with global footprints before they finish college. So are fifty-somethings and boomers who have put off meaningful pursuits for too long. There are more "side hustle" opportunities available to us than ever before. Why go to a bank when you can crowdfund your new Wi-Fi enabled stuffed animal baby monitor in a few days?

In light of the infinite opportunities ripe for the picking, what if we could take the irritating characteristics of our habits of learned helplessness—the sticky, the unconscious, and the unfulfilled parts of our identity—and turn those into money, meaning, and momentum?

What if we could reverse those Cycles of Suck?

Okay, so you now know that diet soda is not helping you lose weight after all. And, worse than that, Martin Seligman was really hard on those poor dogs. But we're sorry to be the bearers of more bad news. As dark as these sound, there's yet another risk right around the corner. It's one you can't afford to overlook, and one that lies at the heart of a brighter future.

3

FIND THE HEART OF YOUR TALENTS

"Most people think they know what they're good at. They are usually wrong. More often, people know what they're not good at—and even then more people are wrong than right."

—Peter F. Drucker

Well done.

With the previous two chapters finished, you've now leveled up with how to think about personal and career risk, hidden or otherwise. But there's another risk with which you probably aren't familiar.

The Risk of Learned Blindness will define your entire life and your capacity for productivity and happiness:

When we look for ourselves in the wrong mirrors, we *learn* to be blind to our talents.

Our talents are tantalizingly close, yet we've taught ourselves to stay in the dark by shying away from risk. In vain, we grasp and grope clumsily asking:

What am I good at? What was I meant to do and who was I meant to become?

If we see even the barest outlines of the answers to these questions, the inevitable more money, more meaning, and more momentum are only a question of time.

But without a glimpse of those answers—no matter how hard we toil, how hard we struggle and fight, we are resigned to a simmering dissatisfaction. Perhaps we're not losing outright, but we certainly aren't winning.

All the while, money, meaning, and momentum remain elusive. Out of sight and out of reach.

As the saying goes, "The only way out is through."

Through this chapter.

10,000 Mistakes

In his massively bestselling and eminently readable book *Outliers,* the brilliant author Malcolm Gladwell popularized the work of psychologist K. Anders Ericsson, who demonstrated that world-class achievement in virtually any field could be had by anyone who dedicated 10,000 hours of "deliberate practice." He strongly suggested that innate talent isn't what separates the best from the pretty good—rather it's simple persistence and dedication to practice.

And lest you think he was telling you something you've known since kindergarten—that practice makes perfect—Gladwell, truly a world-class writer himself, endowed this idea with serious gravitas when he deemed it a "rule"—the "10,000-Hour Rule." No doubt you've heard of it. Twenty hours a week for 10 years and you too will be world class in whatever discipline you choose. (You know it's true because it's a rule!)

If you want to be a world-class golfer, just put in your 10,000 hours.

World-class chess player? Just put in your 10,000 hours.

World-class musician or songwriter? That's right, you over there with the tin ear, humming annoyingly out of tune, you can learn to play guitar like Mark Knopfler or write songs like Bob Dylan. Just put in your 10,000 hours

The 10,000-Hour Rule lets us temporarily fantasize what it

might be like to be a world-class writer—like Gladwell is. But when we return to reality, most of us realize that we don't have 10,000 hours to invest toward becoming world-class writers. So we start heading down a path of convenient self-rationalization: The 10,000-Hour Rule says I could be a world-class writer if I did enough deliberate practice in writing. But I don't really have the time for that, with my wife and two kids, my career leading software engineering teams, and that little free time I do have I use to go backpacking in the Sierras. If I did have the time, then I would certainly write and certainly become a world-class novelist because that's what the rule says. The only difference between me and Malcom Gladwell or me and J.K. Rowling is that they both have 10,000 hours in their respective fields. Otherwise, we're totally the same!

Thinking along those lines ignores a fundamental truth, namely that innate talent does matter. Even worse, it willfully ignores the inescapably necessary *self-discovery* of our talents.

The 10,000-Hour Rule has done untold damage to people trying to get more money, more meaning, and more momentum in their lives. Our natural inclination is to perceive ourselves as more skilled and more talented than we really are, and the rule has encouraged people to take unwarranted risks, pursuing talent that they likely will never develop. In the pursuit of mastery, it encourages people to confuse the trophy with the target. But they aren't the same thing. Aim for the trophy and you're practically guaranteed to miss. We call this the Madness of Mastery.

Of course, deliberate practice at the piano, on the basketball court, or writing software *will* improve your skills. As Patrick's childhood judo coach used to say, "Practice doesn't make perfect. Perfect practice makes perfect." But innate talent maintains a central role in ultimate success. No matter how many hours he practices playing the guitar, Patrick will never be a world-class musician. That's not to say that Patrick shouldn't practice guitar and enjoy the process of making music, but he probably shouldn't decide to pour all his money, energy, and focus into becoming a professional musician.

We won't waste time extolling the virtues of hard work. *We know that you know* that hard work is necessary but not alone sufficient for achieving your goals. What we'd like to do is convince you that the success equation that some think looks like this:

Success = hard work x luck

actually looks like:

Success = hustle x luck x your unique talents

Sitting around indulging our baser instincts about what we wish our talents were is wasteful and counterproductive. (Patrick isn't sitting around resenting the fact that he isn't Mark Knopfler.) Wishing we were superstars at something that we're not great at just moves us further away from money, meaning, and momentum. It's negative dreaming about who we wish we were that makes for one of the most unrecoverable and regretful of hidden risks: that we don't ever discover and see and make use of our real talents.

The Fun House Mirrors of Talent Perception

There are countless stories of people who have been misjudged, shunned, and shamed because they didn't fit the preconceived notions of a certain mold.

In our experience, we are equally inclined to overestimate our own talents in some areas while simultaneously undervaluing our abilities in other areas. It's like looking in a fun house mirror—you see a version of yourself that resembles you, but it's so distorted that you really can't use it as a guide. What's worse is that we often let somebody else hold the fun house mirror, and they add to the distortion by moving that mirror around in whatever way suits them best.

In order to start finding and seeing your true talents, you need to understand the two distorted mirrors that are preventing you from seeing your true self: the "Lake Wobegon effect" and the "kangaroo court of talent."

The Lake Wobegon Effect

Humorist Garrison Keillor has made an entire career of poking fun at a particularly interesting facet of the human psyche known as illusory superiority. For his long-running variety-hour radio show *A Prairie Home Companion*, the avuncular Keillor created a fictional town named Lake Wobegon, "where all the women are strong, all the men are good-looking, and all the children are above average."

That cute, counterintuitive hook should put a smile on your face, because our intuition tells us what statistics confirm: It is impossible for all members of a set to be above average across the same dimension.

One real-life demonstration of the Lake Wobegon effect plays out when people are asked to rate their driving ability relative to the rest of the population. Time after time, the vast majority of those polled rate themselves high in driving ability, usually well above average. They're basically saying, "Everyone else is a terrible driver, just not me. I'm amazing."

The Lake Wobegon effect is your ego subconsciously protecting itself from thoughts it has determined to be harmful—in this case, the uncomfortable truth that you are a worse driver than you perceive yourself to be. A speck of self-deception is actually useful. Since we deceive ourselves to deceive others, a classic example of this is over-confidence in business. When others doubt your abilities to deliver, overconfidence can go a long way in assuaging their fears.

But too much self-deception is just plain dangerous.

It is like your immune system kicking in when you get infected with a bug. When you have a foreign substance like a virus or bacteria in your body, you want some temporary protection while your body's natural defenses kick into gear—but if your immune system is switched on at all times and is busy attacking healthy tissue, you're suffering from an autoimmune disorder.

And when it comes to accurately judging your own hidden talents, Lake Wobegon's overzealous, nonstop protective effect of hiding the truth—maybe an ugly truth—from your ego becomes your worst enemy.

The Kangaroo Court of Talent

Just as we often overestimate our abilities in a field in which we want to succeed, human nature also inclines us to let ourselves be judged harshly by people who have no business weighing in on our dreams. We call these people the kangaroo court of talent.

The ability to accurately judge any sort of talent, especially hidden talent, is rare indeed. Looking at patterns in ostensibly objective data can help identify undervalued talent that our human biases have probably missed. The kangaroo court of talent certainly missed NFL quarterback Tom Brady. Brady wasn't drafted until the sixth round of the 2000 NFL draft. That's an ignominious beginning for a player who, at the time of this writing, has been Super Bowl MVP three times and has won the same contest an incredible four times.

The fundamental truth is that for a great many things in our lives, just as we ourselves are remarkably bad at judging our own talents, other people—often in positions of power—are usually even worse.

All too frequently, when we self-judge, we unfairly interrogate our talents in front of a kangaroo court whose goal is not justice or under-standing but humiliation, fear, and punishment. That jury is not peo-pled by sage philosopher-kings who have our long-term interests in mind but by flawed everyday folks, just like us, who have their own interests at hand, whether consciously or unconsciously.

Among those who sit on this jury are our often well-intentioned parents, who have their own insecurities and regrets about their lives—their terrible demons that have nothing to do with us. They make no effort to understand us yet they sit in judgment. Next to them are the social-status makers, who will only deliver a verdict that conforms to society's collective understanding of success. Got an offbeat talent that doesn't match those of being a doctor, lawyer, or investment banker?

Fuggedaboutit.

Our friends and peers are too busy competing with us to be depended upon for reliable feedback about our talents. And in fact, on occasion, they will even give in to the devil on their shoulder to undercut us and demoralize us.* Forgive them, for they know not what they do.

Our point here isn't to demonize those who love you—your friends and family and colleagues—but to point out an inevitable conclusion: You yourself must determine what your talents and abilities are, and you need to do it by understanding that reflections in the fun house mirrors are inevitably distorted and won't reveal your true talents.

There are considerably more wrong ways than right ways to do this. Wrong ways include "figuring out your why," which ostensibly surfaces your real motivations and then serves as a compass for the rest of your life. Or taking multiple-choice career tests that promise to render an accurate psychological profile that suggests the best career options for you. Or even asking "smart people" their opinions about you.

Pulling Punches on Overmatched Opponents

Neil's childhood friend Bibiana is a visual artist of some talent, but she's entirely miserable. It was clear from a young age that Bibiana has artistic talents. Even as a kindergartner, her parents could always distinguish her finger paintings from those of her classmates. Among the entirely indecipherable mess of cuteness tacked to the classroom wall, there was always one finger painting that looked nothing like the rest. It wasn't necessarily that it was a faithful representation of some

---

* As an early reader of this book remarked, "This is exactly why you should never go shopping for your wedding dress with your best friend." Indeed.

object, but the composition, the color choices, the proportions and symmetries were undeniably artistic, and orders of magnitude better than what the average kindergartner was capable of. Growing up, Bibiana flirted with her talent. For prom, she designed a dress inspired by the one worn by Jessica Rabbit in *Who Framed Roger Rabbit*. In college, she sculpted and carved models and learned the basics of oil painting, but, ultimately, she never really committed to further developing her talents.

She claimed to want to sharpen her talents. But enter that art contest? Nah, too commercial. Find an apprenticeship with an industrial design team? Uh-uh. She never felt qualified. Maybe display some work in the coffee shop down the street? That's so lame. Besides, who would want to buy her paintings? Whatever the case, Bibi always found an excuse to pull her punches.

She pulled her punches against opponents she could have easily overwhelmed, and in some cases even knocked out. The one time she did step into the ring, to participate in a public art exhibition that involved painting a 7-foot-tall sculpture of a trout for display at the local post office, she won wide acclaim in her hometown for her highly evocative and imaginative painting of a fly fisherman on the trout itself.

While her artistic talents were off the charts, her written and verbal talents were strictly average. Yet, after college, she became obsessed with applying to law school. For anyone unaware, in law school, you compete with driven people whose verbal, written, and communication skills are off the charts.

Instead of getting into the right ring that would have allowed her natural talents to shine and excel, Bibiana kept trying to get into rings in which she was clearly overmatched, and in doing so she ended up suffering humiliating defeats and setbacks.

Ironically, Bibiana knows what her talents are, but she continues in her refusal to harness them. Hired and fired, hired and fired, she cycles through temporary administrative jobs and is stuck in a never-ending Cycle of Suck.

But most of us don't even know where to start. The longer we wait on figuring out what we were meant to do, the more likely it is that we too will go on to make the same two types of mistakes that Bibiana made: getting in the ring with someone we shouldn't or pulling our punches to avoid the easy knockout.

Both of these leave us without money, without meaning, and without momentum. We're left only with what-ifs, would'ves, could'ves, and should'ves.

We need to know our talents to know which rings to enter.

Unseen Job Descriptions

Ever see a job description that seems to map to you perfectly? Ever interview and even get hired for that very job only to find out that your dream job is absolutely nothing like the job description? If your self-perception is like a fun house mirror, then the hiring process is like a trick can that you think will be filled with peanuts but when you open it up, a goofy snake pops out.

Job descriptions are insidious creatures designed to capture and fool us. They bait us with a description of the roles of a job in the most superficial way, and in doing so they hide from us the real truths of the job. Even as we make our best efforts to move ahead on the career path we want to pursue, we are prevented from matching our talents with the responsibilities we think we are signing on for.

A job description for a COO might include the following:

- Oversee all aspects of manufacturing operations including design, engineering, purchasing, project management, and assembly.
- Serve as an active, resourceful, decisive member of the executive team.
- Spearhead increase in manufacturing capacity.

The same job description rewritten to reflect the reality of the position—and the description that would be more useful to you— would be:

- Make sure we manufacture our products efficiently no matter how many bad decisions our CEO makes.

A job description for a mechanical engineer might look like:

- Proficient in latest AutoCAD software.
- Good at client communication.

Written to accurately reflect the job, this might read:

- Babysit overqualified and underpaid team of burned-out engineers.
- Cajole, bribe, and threaten engineers to ensure that our products won't explode when manufactured overseas.

No need to belabor the point, eh?

The job description that we respond to is clear and easy to understand but ultimately masks what the job *really* entails. Job descriptions are akin to icebergs: Most of the substance sits below the surface. The rewritten job description tells you what is hidden but really matters.

As a hustler, you will make it a habit to see the unseen and feel the undercurrents, and you must always decode and *go beyond the job description*. Since the truths are hidden below, you'll learn why and how to expose that substance and build a "Proofberg," as we'll discuss in Chapter 13.

Most people never learn this. Patrick, himself a late bloomer, grokked this, painfully, rather late in life.

Who's Eating Risk?

Around 2007, a friend of Patrick's was astounded to learn that Patrick was leaving a well-paid job to found a start-up. Lack of a steady income stream, lack of direction, and lack of job security made it impossible for this person to conceive that anyone might leave a "sure thing" for something riskier, even if it was more meaningful or interesting.

Uncomfortably, Patrick knew that his friend wasn't wrong . . . logically. But Patrick had begun to pay attention to his own successes and failures at the jobs he had held.

Once Patrick stopped looking at his reflection in fun house mirrors, a distinct pattern began to emerge: Patrick was never promoted at the same rates as his colleagues, even though his technical skills were as good if not better than theirs. Patrick's strengths lay in synthesizing seemingly unrelated ideas and organizing them into technology to do useful things. When he was given autonomy to make decisions—and mistakes—Patrick performed extremely well. But there was always some unspoken friction between Patrick and his bosses. They accused Patrick of being like a stubborn mule. If Patrick felt like working in the direction indicated by his bosses, he did well. But too often, Patrick held ideas contrary to management's direction. Unlike many of his colleagues, not avoiding failure wasn't enough for Patrick; he had to feel he was striving to win.

The battle between logic and emotion that raged inside Patrick was not easy to bear. But once he made the difficult decision to leave his position, he felt great relief.

A short while after Patrick left, his former company went through an unexpected downsizing, and those who remained, like Patrick's friend, had to endure the salmonella of a 30 percent salary cut. At the same time, Patrick had leveled up in real-world business experience in one-tenth of the time it would have taken him to do so at his old company. Patrick also ended up self-publishing his first book, which led to a traditional book deal and eventually a spot on the bestseller list.

Furthermore, Patrick experienced an entirely new set of emotions: the feeling of being able to take advantage of opportunities without having to ask permission, of building up some of his own momentum toward something that made his life feel meaningful.

Some might say that this is nothing more than a question of

toughness. Who's tough enough to grit their teeth through risky or terrible experiences? But that's not quite right. Hustle isn't about toughing it out at all costs. It's about making the best set of choices for the long game. Don't forget, Patrick's old colleague toughed it out, right into a salary cut.

Gritty Little Lies

Get tough or get out. When the going gets tough, the tough get going. Keep fighting. Never ever give up. Never stop. Achieve your dreams no matter the odds. Where there's a will, there's a way. You'll find a way if you try hard enough. Try, try, and try again.

Every single person reading this sentence has heard and said a variant of the above.

Before you go any further in this book, let's get a fundamental misconception out of the way: Today's trendy concept of "grit" is yesterday's "toughness." All manner of psychological studies and anecdata* show that in the face of setbacks, grittier people tend to achieve more of their goals.

And we're not arguing with that. Without a smidgen of a doubt, tenacious people win.

They're hardier and more resilient. Wanna win?

Then you—yeah you, chump—should be grittier. And while you're at it, be braver, be richer, and be better looking, too.

How exactly do I become tougher? you ask yourself. Well, well, well, *mon ami,* that part they don't tell you.

You know what is tough about toughness? Being tough is staying tough when you've FUBAR-ed an important project. Your boss now openly questions your abilities, your colleagues happily throw you under the bus, and as you cower in your cubicle, you helpfully deliver the coup de grâce to yourself: you begin to believe your own bad press.

Toughness is like the old saying about credit: You can't get any when you need it most.

---

* We're making *anecdata* a word.

Of course, the Get Tough choir means well. Yet, when you feel like you're drowning, when you feel like you're barely getting by, there's no light switch to flip that will turn on the hero when you feel like a zero.

It simply doesn't exist.

Trying to do that is akin to playing with one of those silly water wiggler toys—the harder you squeeze, the quicker it jumps out of your hands.

Ever tell an agitated person to "Calm down!"?

How'd that work out for you?

The truth is that grit and success have a paradoxical chicken-and-egg relationship. Which comes first? Does grit always create success? If you cannot be gritty, are you doomed to failure?

Perhaps success breeds grit?

As you may have noticed, it's fairly easy to be "gritty" or "fill-in-your-favorite-synonym-for-tough" when you have six figures laying around in the bank or when your network includes the who's who of the political elite in your city.

It's easy to bargain for a higher salary when you know that your company's competitor has been recruiting you for the past 3 months.

It's easy to fire a high-maintenance, annoying customer when your cash flows are healthy and your profits are fat.

It's easy to get up early in the morning to get a workout in and sip down a green smoothie when you know all is well at the office and at home.

Success begets grit, grit begets success.

While we aim to inspire you in your hustle, this book and our advice are firmly rooted in reality—which is why you won't be reading trite platitudes about tenacity and mental toughness.* Not because they're not true—but because *you already know all you need to know.* We could all benefit from being more tough *blah blah blah.*

Blech!

---

* Well, maybe a few.

Stealing Success

What you may not have realized is that the success you need to be grittier in desperate times doesn't have to be directly related to where you are failing.

When your confidence is shaken at work because that genius marketing campaign you spent 9 months designing ended up bombing, you can tap the motivation needed to (a) shake it off and (b) steal strength from another place in your life that happens to be positive and thriving.

Not only can you, in fact, you *must* steal that success.

Diversification in your personal and professional life is not just about getting the right mix of risk, but about stealing the wonderful side effects of success—like confidence, toughness, and vision—from one part of your life to help drive other parts of your life that could use a jolt of confidence. And there is always a part of our lives that could use improvement.

In the outdated practice of monoculture forestry, forests were managed so that one tree species made up the entire forest. In the end, this made the forest more susceptible to fire and disease. There is similar danger in our hustle being overly focused on one thing; that danger is compounded when that one focus becomes our only identity. After all, we're not monks in a temple meditating 16 hours a day. We can't retreat all the time and still have an impact on the world. We have to be out there mixing it up, falling and failing. That's how we find ourselves—by shaking things up.

Because when we fail and fall—and we all eventually do—that one identity is rarely a strong enough bootstrap itself. That is why our identities need to be like a varied forest, one made up of firs and maples and sequoias and redwoods, which together constitute healthier, more resilient mixed forests that bounce back faster and better from adverse environmental conditions. Multiple, healthy identities make us more resilient because we can top up our success tanks as needed.

These untapped reservoirs of success you've experienced, what we call Proof, could be your family, your network, your hobbies, your honeypots or side-hustle projects. (We'll revisit these in detail in Chapter 13). The successes of these offer that much-needed fuel in your tank when you're being waterboarded with self-doubt Kool-Aid.

But we have to start somewhere. Where do we find these initial successes?

Mirror of Experience

Instead of the fun house mirror, looking at ourselves through a "mirror of experience" lets us see what is legible and what is illegible. We have legible talents (easily seen and communicated, often of medium value) and illegible talents (hard to see, harder to articulate, but incredibly valuable). And the only way to begin to understand and start to leverage our illegible talents is with frequent, varied interactions with a dynamic environment.

So do something. Do something that *moves* you. Do something that excites or energizes you.

Don't talk about it. Don't dream it. Don't plan it.

Don't plan to plan it.

We'll revisit this later, but for the moment, understand that perfection can be perilous and the quest for mastery can lead to madness.

Do something that exposes yourself to novel, challenging projects and environments in your work.

You're Not a Cockroach: Specialization Is for Insects

"A human being should be able to change a diaper, plan an invasion, butcher a hog, conn a ship, design a building, write a sonnet, balance accounts, build a wall, set a bone, comfort the dying, take orders, give orders, cooperate, act alone, solve equations, analyze a new problem, pitch manure, program a computer, cook a tasty meal, fight efficiently, die gallantly. Specialization is for insects."

—Robert Heinlein

Which is exactly why people, young and old, should try lots and lots and lots of different things and not specialize too early. By specializing too early, you self-sabotage and cut off promising avenues of talent exploration, and you take on a terrible hidden risk of never knowing your personal gifts, your personal drivers of money, meaning, and momentum, your true, illegible talents.

Self-Diagnosing Talent Exercise

The only way to get an accurate read on what you were born to do is to follow an exceedingly simple and ancient practice popularized by management theorist Peter F. Drucker (whom we quoted at the beginning of this chapter). Before you start a new project or venture, write down your expectations about what you think that project will entail from you, what you will be asked to give and do. After the project ends, record the results. Was it a success or a failure? What did you do well? What did you do poorly? What did you find yourself doing or feeling that you didn't know you were capable of? What were some quirky things you did or said that helped bring about a successful end?

By recording and revisiting your reality, you can look into the mirror of experience and see yourself as you truly are, thus avoiding the distorting reflections of the Lake Wobegon effect and the kangaroo court of talent.

If you do this consistently—yes, you have to put in a little time for it—a distinct and unique pattern will surface. This pattern will reveal your strengths and your weaknesses, your unconscious behaviors and your true talents—talents that were equally as illegible to you as they were to others.

Once you see the surprising outlines of your strengths that begin to reveal themselves to you, savor that day—for most people never even get close to understanding what they are great at. After that, you must do everything in your power to improve upon and better your strengths.

Are you great at persuading people to take action? Take classes in pitching, sales, and extemporaneous speaking. An exceptional seller of ideas, products, and services is worth their weight in gold to any organization.

Are you good at engineering solutions to hard technical problems? Join teams doing mentally exhausting and complex technical work.

Are you bad at reading others' emotional states? Avoid highly coordinated, collaborative work that requires you to manage other's emotional states and needs.

Identifying your talents and then improving your strengths is the simplest and single best step anyone can take. Yet most never will.

Why not? Because they're too focused on avoiding failure. Because seeing your talents in the mirror of experience requires doing, and anything worth doing involves a four-letter word.

The Four-Letter Word You Need More of in Your Life

We mentioned in Chapter 1 that if you're not owning your dream and working to direct your own destiny, you're paying rent into someone else's. So it should come as no surprise that this leaves you feeling less than fulfilled. Your soul knows you're on the wrong path even if you yourself cannot find the words to express the root of your meh.

The good news is this can be treated. So how do you start? We crave it, and even obsess about it. So what is it? The filthiest four-letter word you can think of is *R-I-S-K*.

Most of us equate risk with danger—something to be avoided altogether. But think of risk like oxygen. It's neither good nor bad. It's essential and inescapable. Either too much or too little can harm you, but no matter, as a human, you're already breathing oxygen and taking risks everyday just by being alive. It's unavoidable. And just like food, you can make better choices about the risks you choose to consume.

How More Risk Means Less Risk

It is helpful to think about risk in our personal lives and careers the same way Wall Street thinks about risk in stocks. Roughly speaking, there are two types of risks in the stock market. The first type, "idio-syncratic risk," means that there is a chance that *something*—maybe it's good, maybe it's bad—happens with any one company. Good news! The company has figured out a way to allow you to carry all of your music with you in your pocket. You're so smart for having bought Apple stock! Uh oh! The CEO has been cooking the books and the company is going bankrupt. Shouldn't have bought that Enron stock! That's idiosyncratic risk.

The second type of risk, "market risk," reflects the broader risk that all companies face. The economy is booming, so people want to buy more stuff. Great! Stocks go up. There's a terrorist attack that devastates a major city. Horrible! Stocks go down.

If you hold enough risk in your stock portfolio, you actually don't bear any idiosyncratic risk. If something bad happens to one stock, others likely benefit. For example, when oil prices spike, the transpor-tation companies in your portfolio might suffer, but the energy com-panies in your portfolio will surely benefit. This sort of risk diversification is exactly what top-tier investment firms do. They buy *more* total risk to take on less downside risk. This means that, theo-retically, the more risks you take in the market, the *less* risky investing actually is overall.

Look at the risk we have in our own lives. When it comes to our life choices, a lack of appetite for the right type of risk makes us *unhealthy*. We must take on the *right* type of risk to develop options. We're not advocating you strap into a flying squirrel suit and jump off the edge of a Norwegian fjord so you can glide along a ridgeline at Mach 3. Rather, we are saying that you should take on the right type of risk and develop upside optionality, the ability to capture and profit from random fortuitous events.

For those of us who work in large organizations, we must ask these questions: What are we missing by not taking on that challeng-ing project? What are the opportunity costs of not getting a promo-tion, or of not even fighting for one? How might we benefit by going that extra mile, staying a few hours later, and buttoning up a project extra tight? What if we swam against the corporate cultural tide in our efforts to defend an intriguing yet unproven product? What if in a moment when we felt suffocated by our colleagues' silent judgments we tried to blaze our own path instead of joining the herd?

The more right risk we take on, the more our downside risk diminishes as we answer the questions we put to ourselves when we look in the mirror of experience.

The Pursuit of Perfection Hinders Your Hustle

As we've hinted at, there is one additional secret we need to tell you: Your hustle isn't about becoming a more perfect, invincible superhero-genius impervious to all the pain and drama life throws at you.

This outcome is unrealistic and unattainable, and it perverts the reason for hustling to begin with. You don't hustle to be perfect. Your quirks and your imperfections are what make your hustle more powerful and unique. Hustling is where you learn what you love *and* love what you learn.

The Perils of Perfection are like quicksand. We're knee deep and sinking fast. The clock is ticking, but we stand unmoving, planning to plan the most perfect-*est* escape. Doing our best to avoid failure we sink deeper into indecision. And the next thing we know, the alarm clock rings, and another year has come and gone.

When all we really needed to do was to take a step—any move, however imperfect or messy or simple—to keep from being bogged down in the swamps of yesterday.

Because perfection tends to make us more risk averse, the landlords want us to become perfectionists. Yet the right risk in the right amount is healthy. It motivates us to discover success and in doing so extinguishes the Mediocrity of Meh. As General George S. Patton once remarked, "A good plan violently executed now is better than a perfect plan executed next week."

Hustle is about the small everyday wins, not the galactic shifts. The gift of imperfection is that you can learn to rewire and retool along the way. Your hustle, the way you maintain momentum and move forward, is a virtuous cycle. For as you hustle more, you'll find that you encounter more good luck. That good luck will only add to your momentum, which will in turn create more opportunity.

Yes, you will get luckier, but before you throw on your ascot and collect the much-deserved billion-dollar lottery payout, sometimes you have to embrace a few small doses of pain. But fear not, this is pain that brings you gains and transforms your life.

PART TWO
HEAD

"In order to change the world you have to get your head together first."

—JIMI HENDRIX

4

SMALL DOSES OF PAIN

"The best people all have some kind of scar."

—Kiera Cass

Saving a Princess

In our favorite scene from the cult classic film *The Princess Bride*, the handsome blond protagonist, Westley, challenges the crafty villain Vizzini—who is holding the object of Westley's affection, the beautiful Princess Buttercup, hostage at knifepoint—to a battle of wits "to the death." (If you're unfamiliar with the film, *The Princess Bride* is a hilarious satire of the fairy-tale and adventure story genres.)

To commence the battle of wits, Vizzini pours two goblets of wine as Westley sits down across from him. Once seated, Westley presents a vial filled with a powder for Vizzini to sniff, and matter-of-factly, Westley explains, "What you do not smell is called iocaine powder. It is odorless, tasteless, dissolves instantly in liquid, and is among the more deadly poisons known to man."

As Vizzini watches bemusedly, Westley picks up both wine goblets and turns his back to obscure them from Vizzini's view. Westley slyly glances back at Vizzini before presenting both goblets and asking melodramatically, "All right. Where is the poison? The battle of wits has begun."

The scene then segues into a hilarious sequence of Vizzini trying to triple-quadruple-quintuple-reverse-psychology Westley in an effort to figure out which goblet contains the poisoned wine.

Clearly frustrated, Vizzini distracts Westley with a "What's that over there?!" prompting Westley to turn away, allowing Vizzini to swap the goblets. Then, Vizzini announces he is ready to drink. Both Westley and Vizzini take hearty swigs, after which Westley deadpans to Vizzini, "You guessed wrong."

Cackling gleefully, Vizzini explains to Westley that he had *switched* goblets when Westley was distracted. Moments later, in midchortle, Vizzini keels over, dead. Princess Buttercup, who had been sitting blindfolded next to Vizzini during the entire "battle of wits," comments, "And to think, all that time it was *your* cup that was poisoned."

To which Westley smugly responds, "They were both poisoned. I spent the last few years building up an immunity to iocaine powder."

Delighting in Small Doses of Pain

Now, if you were lucky enough to have a teacher in school share a bit of strategic thinking or perhaps even some "game theory," you have the tools to win a "battle of wits to the death." To do so, you need to create a combination of best-response strategies by reasoning backward through the decision tree of your opponent.

You can be Vizzini—the smartest man on Earth. And if you're Vizzini, guess what? You're still dead, no matter how brilliant your strategy, because Westley executed the ultimate hustle. He embraced the risk of the poison and spent years anticipating this type of showdown. When it finally came, he was prepared because he had built up resistance to the deadly iocaine poison in a scientific process known as hormesis. He started out by taking a small risk that then got bigger and bigger as his immunity grew, and when the opportunity arrived, he was more than ready.

Here's why hormesis and hustle go so well together: Hormesis shows that repeated exposures to small doses of stressors and risk don't weaken but, surprisingly, *strengthen* our biological systems.

The Benefits of Body Damage

Exercise is a good example of small doses of pain. When we exercise vigorously, lift heavy weights, or engage in challenging resistance training, we take on a bit of risk and do a small bit of damage to our muscles. Our muscles suffer "microtraumas," and our bodies respond by renovating and bolstering the traumatized muscle tissue. As our muscles grow, we experience temporary, albeit acute, small doses of pain. In the long run, these lead to gains in strength, endurance, energy, and vitality, and to better physical appearance, self-esteem, and confidence. Exercise is never much fun at the time we do it, but it affords us huge benefits. Simple association with the promise of exercise—better health—is the reason so many of us join a gym and pay a monthly fee but never actually go. Too little exercise and we don't grow. Not only that, but it's crushingly boring. Infrequently exercising, or frequently exercising but not pushing your body, is like playing level one of a video game over and over and over again. That's why a trainer will typically make you do many different types of exercises. On the other hand, too much exercise can lead to long-term damage to your body.

Finding the right level of exercise for small doses of pain is the key. Our bodies become stronger in response to a dose of mildly stressful exercise. And as we grow stronger, we can increase that dose by lifting heavier weights or adding sprints to our running routine. In other words, we can ultimately level up.

This is precisely why senior citizens are advised to lift weights and maintain active lifestyles, as it helps them combat osteoporosis. It's also why injured athletes are encouraged to get back on their feet and in motion doing rehabilitation as soon as they are able to move their injured muscles and joints.

As much as small doses of pain are about growth, they're also about preventing atrophy. A common manifestation of atrophy is when a child has a cast removed from his leg. The muscles on the previously injured leg are significantly smaller and weaker than those on the other leg. The muscles have atrophied due to lack of use. Here again, exercise is almost always prescribed to reverse this effect. It is plain to see that our bodies respond well to managed doses of stressors. In fact, our bodies *thrive* on them.

This is applicable to our careers as well. If you hate speaking in public, what's the cure? Your landlord will tell you to chill out and pop a Xanax. But that's sure to keep you from ever growing past the point that you're at now. A much better idea would be to seek out small doses of pain. Start by giving a 15-second speech at the dinner table— a simple toast. If just thinking about that right now is making your heart pound—*good!* That's the point. Do it every night until you're bored with it. Like Ahnold tells us, "No pain, no gain." Surfacing your talents will make you distinctly uncomfortable at times. That's good. If it doesn't hurt a little, you're not moving forward.

The Benefits of Brain Damage

Another somewhat mysterious wonder of small doses of pain concerns what happens in our brains on a day-to-day basis. With more than 85 billion neurons and even more support cells, called glia, our brains are bundled juggernauts of possibility.

Remember what they taught you in eighth-grade health class when they were teaching you to say no to drugs, *mmmmkay?* They told you that you were born with a finite number of brain cells, and every time you killed one of those cells—whether it was by banging your head in the mosh pit or guzzling a funnel of Milwaukee's Best—there was no way to get it back.

Well, guess what. They lied. Shocking, isn't it?

Brain cells continue growing throughout our lives. The catch here, of course, is that our brain cells don't grow without effort. That ability for growth is known as neuroplasticity. Growth occurs when we engage in cognitive activities, such as when we learn a new language, acquire a new technical or creative skill set, have a novel experience, take on a new challenge in unfamiliar territory, or solve a complex challenge. (Think of those situations where you need to "herd cats," like when you're bringing a new product to market.) The pain we feel in our minds is helping, not harming us.

Language works as a particularly potent example. Mastering a foreign tongue benefits us greatly in the short term. We learn new phrases, like how to say "I love you!" in Spanish (¡Te Amo!), or ask "Pardon me, but is that your dog peeing on my lawn?" in Hungarian.

But learning a new language is often an intensely frustrating exercise, as we struggle to shape our tongues and lips to accurately pronounce foreign sounds, to remember foreign concepts of time, and to recall odd grammar structures that are without equivalents in our native language—all in an effort to save ourselves embarrassment. But those tiny, repeated frustrations transform into long-term advantages. As we, sometimes painfully, sharpen our minds and learn to "code switch" in and out of our native tongue and the new language, we create a kind of neural fortitude. The more we practice our new modes of expression, the more we might be able to bolster our neurological health and recovery and delay the onset of traumatic brain diseases like Alzheimer's. In fact, recent research suggests that bilingual people tend to recover from strokes twice as fast as people who speak only one language.

Just a few days after Jonas experienced a stroke, he began a personal battery of unusual acts of hormesis of his own choosing that included everything from reading books in Spanish to brushing his teeth with his left (nondominant) hand to doing sophisticated math problems and crossword puzzles to spelling challenging words, like *Czechoslovakia*, backward. Jonas did each of these for a few minutes every day for a few months, mostly in secret. He feared others— especially coworkers at his company—would think the stroke and his subsequent cognitive challenges had gotten the best of him. These exercises helped Jonas regain confidence in his mental faculties, and he credits them with speeding his recovery.

Of course, another application of hormesis is in our careers, where to succeed we must stay on top of a blistering array of tasks at any given moment on any given day: new business, customer-relations challenges, technology issues, creative opportunities, cash flow management, marketing campaigns, planning, and scheduling. Because of this, we must hustle ourselves into "mindfields," areas in which we lack expertise, some of which will be uncomfortable.

Inherently, stretching occurs here, and the benefit of our discomfort is small doses of gain—in increased learning, in experiences and familiarity with a new task or subject—that enable new synapses or connections in the brain.

When it comes to our brains, small doses of pain pay us back in spades. And just like muscles can be retrained after serious injury, so, too, our brain tissue expands in new ways as we pursue knowledge and previously unfamiliar experiences. This is a good type of brain damage.

Whether body damage or brain damage, life is an incremental process of growth. And we can apply the same process of hormesis to countless aspects of our life and work, whether it's leading a team, learning a new language, launching a product, or anything else we might think of.

We actually *need* small amounts of pain to make gains to prevent our existing skills from atrophying, to grow our future skills and knowledge, and to anticipate and solve complex challenges.

And, paramount, we need to take small, manageable risks that, in aggregate, de-risk your downside risk profile and create upside potential wherever you may take your hustle. See—we just spoke a foreign language there. In English, that last sentence translates to "Good things happen when you take more risks."

Big Pain, No Gain

If your hustle is all-pain-nothing-but-pain, you're just a sadist, and you're doing it wrong.

All you macho men and macho women reading this book—please take to heart that we have described hormesis as requiring *small* doses of pain. If you push yourself too far beyond your abilities and identities, you don't see any gain from that pain. And that pain can be too much to handle.

With hormesis, the message isn't "Whatever doesn't kill me only makes me stronger" but "The dose makes the poison." What we perceive as small is relative to the doer of the deed. So be sensible about it.

Prescription: Your Daily Dose of Pain

You must make sure to build incrementally so that you can get back on your horse and not get trampled underneath. For this, we suggest a "daily dose of pain."

Look in the mirror and think to yourself, What is the smallest thing I could do today to reap a long-term hormetic benefit? All it has to be is (a) small, (b) slightly annoying or odd, and (c) gainful or promising in some way.

Ten real-life examples you could start today include:

1. If you're out of shape, try to do 10 pushups or 5 minutes of yoga every day this week.

2. Know that coworker you cannot stand, the super-annoying loud-talker who won't leave your cubicle and constantly disrupts your work with her boring stories about her husband or her kids? Find something truly virtuous about her and compliment her sincerely.

3. Do you always order the same sandwich at your favorite café? Ask the waiter to surprise you with a dealer's choice. The waiter chooses an entrée without informing you, and you promise yourself you will eat it and even try to taste a few specific ingredients, no matter what he chooses. (This is exactly how Patrick learned that he loves Brussels sprouts.)

4. Find a different route home from work for a week straight.

5. Hold a conversation with a few friends and never mention "me" or "I" or "my."

6. Go to a movie on a Friday night *by yourself.*

7. When you find yourself listening to a friend trying to convince you of the merits of one of their ideas, resist the urge to cross your arms. (It's harder than you might think.)

8. Learn one new word every day. And use it at least 10 times that day.

9. Instead of heading straight into work, wake up an hour early and go for a walk.

10. Take a walk around your neighborhood and look for three new things you haven't ever noticed before.

Something, no matter how small a pain, is always better than nothing. The point isn't to punish or deny ourselves but to gently prod ourselves to grow a teeny, tiny bit every day, so that one day we'll be ready to save a princess or prince ourselves.

Aside from the hormetic benefits of small doses of pain, there is another major unseen benefit.

So tell us, are you feeling lucky, punk?

5

MANUFACTURING LUCK

"We hold these truths to be self-evident, that all people are created equal, endowed with certain inalienable rights . . . Among these are Life, Liberty, Luck and the Pursuit of Happiness."
—The Forefathers of America (purportedly from an early draft of the Declaration of Independence)

Luck in a Creek

Patrick was happily enduring a hot and humid spring afternoon with his son, Shane, tramping around together in a wilderness preserve not far from their home in Austin, Texas. This preserve's main feature is an idyllic creek bordered by verdant, low-slung oak trees overhanging its limestone banks. The area is home to all sorts of fauna, from fat tadpoles to stealthy coyotes and even the occasional snake.

Atop a thick, moss-covered limestone ledge, Shane tightly grasped his plastic 5-gallon bucket within which lurked a heavy coil of twine and an odiferous hunk of bacon. The towheaded Shane carefully, soundlessly surveyed the clear water for any sign of crayfish.

With his hand on Shane's shoulder, Patrick knelt down and peered into the creek's rocky, leaf-littered bottom. A few moments later, as he stood up, Patrick explained in the way only dads can explain the patently obvious, "Shane, I don't see any crayfish here today. I think we're out of luck, bud."

Shane released the bucket and jumped from the mossy ledge into the shallow water. Looking down, he shuffled his feet through the underwater piles of rotting oak leaves, giggling delightedly as dozens of crayfish, hitherto invisible, exploded out from underneath his sandals. With a smile as wide as the creek itself, Shane looked up at his surprised father, still on the bank, and explained joyfully, "You just have to jump in and move around to see them, Daddy."

Beaming as he met Shane's gaze, Patrick felt his proud heart swell as it dawned on him that the 4-year-old student had become the master, and he had taught his father an important lesson about hustle and manufacturing luck.

Manufacturing Luck

In the course of choosing to hustle, it quickly becomes necessary to come to grips with the idea that maybe luck isn't some mystical, capricious force beyond our reach after all. How did Shane find crayfish that Patrick didn't see? How did Westley prepare himself for his big opportunity? Ask yourself, Is it much of a stretch to see a link between our survival, our success, and . . . our luck? We might even suggest they are connected in the most primal, intimate, and practical of ways. There's an evolutionary nature to luck. It serves our desires as a vast reservoir of infinitely available fuel for one purpose: to propel us forward. Further, we might argue that luck bubbles up from deep within our DNA, leaving its markings on human history.

At the intersection of hustle and luck, a universal truth emerges: Choosing to own our dreams teaches us how to run out of unluck. Our commitments make us luckier. Frankly, we care more about the dreams we own than the dreams we rent. And that makes us more likely to fight for what is right and what is ours. This puts us in a long-term position to both manifest and take advantage of more luck the more we gain momentum for the work and life of our preferred designs.

Ejection Seats Are Unlucky

A famous film critic and director once said, "To make a film is to make a mistake." This was especially true for legendary director Francis Ford Coppola. At about the same time Sylvester Stallone was at work on *Rocky,* Coppola found himself on the other side of the world working on an incendiary story set in the jungles of Southeast Asia.

After filming the first two *Godfather* films, this was Coppola's attempt at another modern cinema masterpiece. Yet *Apocalypse Now* had violently self-destructed. A surprise typhoon had completely destroyed his film's set in the Philippines, pushing the film months off schedule and millions over budget. Coppola's actors were too drunk or too high to know their lines, and that was when they weren't in open rebellion against the young director. Not only were millions of Coppola's own dollars at stake, but his reputation and career as a director were on the line as well.

During filming, Coppola wrote in a letter to himself: "My nerves are shot. My heart is broken. My imagination is dead. I have no self-reliance. But like a child just want someone to rescue me."

Coppola made a fateful decision: He could have, with all justification, walked away from the disastrous film production. Yet even though he desperately wanted to, he didn't hit the eject button. It wasn't because he didn't want to give up. He did. It wasn't because he believed in himself. He didn't. It wasn't because he felt bold or trusted his instincts. Neither was the case. He kept pushing forward with the film because there was nothing else to do but keep hustling. And that is when his unluck was about to run out.

During the frenzied creative journey we're all on, at some point we start putting the pieces together and find that nothing fits. The start-up you just launched cannot get a bug-free product out the door. The ad campaign you spent millions of dollars on tests horrifically with your target market. Your silver-tongued salesman managed to sell you but not any actual customers. You're out of money, out of blood, sweat, and tears, and worst of all, you're out of time. Game over.

At about that moment, more than anything we just want someone to come and save us. If there were an eject button, we would have pushed it by then. When everything is falling apart, including ourselves, why do we persevere in extreme adversity to finish the work we've set out to do?

Neil had lost a million dollars by the time he was 21, one hell of a deep hole at such a young age. Jonas had a massive stroke in his twenties while working a demanding job at a start-up. Patrick quit his job without any prospects lined up and with a baby on the way.

The rest of the story of the production of *Apocalypse Now* is history: The actors ended up giving stellar performances, the many rewrites of the script paid off, and the film won multiple Academy Awards. And it was all because Coppola was hell-bent on crossing the finish line, because he knew that momentum makes luck. Behind every creative venture, tough project, work opportunity, start-up, film, book, music, or media project is almost always a story of total disaster, crippling defeat, and soul-crushing despair.

Francis Ford Coppola doubled down on what he knew best: making luck through momentum. In the end, he created a masterpiece of cinema that wouldn't exist today had he not run out of unluck.

And finally, let's not forget, it was the ejection seat that killed Goose in *Top Gun*.

The Science of Luck

It is a commonly held belief that luck, chance, and good fortune are entirely random events or even manifestations of some mystical force. In this way of thinking, some people are just luckier than others. This worldview is captured in sayings like "Right place, right time" or "It's better to be lucky than good" or "Count your lucky stars." We take a different tack.

The work of neuroscientist Dr. James Austin suggests that there are four distinct types of luck. By simply hustling, moving, and doing, we can harvest more good fortune and capture serendipity more regularly. Dr. Austin's classifications of luck fall into these categories, which we've rechristened in the parlance of hustlers.

Type 1: Random Luck. This is what many people call dumb luck, the kind that happens without any effort or influence on your part. Think of it as a gift. You're 45 minutes late and you cringe as you pull into an overcrowded parking lot at a hip music festival. As Florence and the Machine rock the stage, you and 3,000 of your closest friends circle the tiny dirt lot slowly, stalking open parking spots. Hopelessly, you turn a corner and find a wide-open empty spot right next to the concert entrance with nary a car in sight. You squeal like a $2\frac{1}{2}$-year-old on Christmas Day as you cannot believe your luck.

Type 2: Hustle Luck. This is the kind of luck that's created by your momentum and motion. Like 4-year-old Shane, when we stop standing still and "stir up the pot," random ideas are able to surface, get mashed up together, and recombine in new, interesting ways. Some of them will lead to success in solving various everyday challenges or in achieving goals. A conversation at a coffee shop leads to a job interview. Your self-published book brings you a traditional book deal. You call up a customer and they're inspired by your knowledge, requesting you to do private consulting work with their team.

In Neil's case, striking up conversations with random people in the elevators at the Mandarin Oriental in Las Vegas (where he owns a condo) led to multiple "lucky" business deals worth hundreds of thousands of dollars. Neil could have, like most people, remained elevator-mute—doing his best to avoid eye contact and conversation with his fellow passengers. But instead Neil made an effort to connect with the people around him, and, naturally, his enthusiasm for his work came spilling out because it's so integral to who he is. That's how Hustle Luck works.

Don't wait for certainty before taking action. Do something. Anything. Most important is movement; don't ruminate. For Hustle Luck, even random motion is better than standing still. Think of the expression "You've gotta be in it to win it."

Type 3: Hidden Luck. These are the camouflaged opportunities that silently tiptoe in and out of your life each and every day, unnoticed by the unlooking unlucky. This kind of luck can be summed up by the saying "Chance favors only the prepared mind." It's the luck that is generated by creative synthesis of past experiences. It evolves into the realization that you are the only one who understands an open secret. Much of this sort of luck depends on how well prepared you are in your field of inquiry, trade, or discipline and how sensitive and open you are to changes in the world. It's surprisingly easy to train yourself to keep your eyes open for opportunity.

One of the most visible modern examples of a hustler using hidden luck is storyteller Casey Neistat. Casey is a high school dropout who today enjoys what seems like a blessed career creating incredible branded videos for clients such as Nike, Mercedes-Benz, and Google, while simultaneously growing a loyal audience of millions on YouTube. His distinctive, funny video storytelling is an honest reflection of himself, one that is built on his unabashed love for filmmaking. In his words, "I have 60-plus videos on YouTube and over 30 million views. Of those 60, only 3 or 4 are branded videos. I built that audience by telling stories the way I like to tell them."

Before finding success on YouTube with his viral videos, some of which individually boast up to 17 million views, Casey was just another poorly paid videographer hustling for jobs in New York City shooting weddings, graduations, kids' birthday parties, anything that involved picking up a camera. In 2006, Casey and his brother, Van, filmed a few videos for a man named Tom Scott. Tom fell in love with their work and financed a project for the Neistat brothers to create eight 25-minute episodes about their lives. When Casey subsequently sold that show to HBO for $2 million, he had come across a major inflection point in his career. Casey himself claims that meeting Tom and creating the show was just luck and has remarked, "Luck is where opportunity meets preparation."

We agree. But it's even more than that. Casey didn't come across this inflection point; his hustle created it. It's the fourth type of luck, Quirky Luck.

Type 4: Quirky Luck. This is the type of luck that seeks you out because of your inherent weirdness. Many biographers of the famous and infamous have commented on their subjects' eccentricities or odd personal lifestyles. For example, Albert Einstein was known to play his violin as he bird-watched, crying all the while. Charles Dickens combed his hair hundreds of times a day. Benjamin Franklin took daily nude "air baths." Casey Neistat, quite frankly, is an odd-looking guy with a square jaw, a boxer's nose, and coarse, kinky hair. He bears an uncanny resemblance to Bill from the 1980s goofball film *Bill & Ted's Excellent Adventure.* Casey does goofball things, too, like sneaking into a German water park at 2:00 a.m., or flying 27 hours across the world from New York City to Cape Town, South Africa, to surprise his then girlfriend (now wife) Candace, unannounced and recording the entire incident on a video to be shared on YouTube.

We scratch our heads and laugh at these funny quirks now, understanding that these odd habits are a differentiating feature, not a bug. It's not that these people became successful and lucky *despite* their odd habits; it's *because of* their odd habits that they've enjoyed certain idiosyncratic successes. When Hustle Luck and Hidden Luck hook up, Quirky Luck is born. When people do seemingly strange things, they sense, encounter, and accept novel, strange luck.

If you have "weird" interests or odd habits not understood by the conformist status quo, indulge them; don't rein them in. When you embrace who you are, what you do, and how you are different, you leverage your energy, your hustle to create a powerful, organic momentum. Compare that to the energy drain someone experiences trying to fit into a landlord's mold.

So go ahead, let your freak flag fly. We promise that you'll get luckier.

Accepting that luck is, to a greater or lesser extent, a constant in life should give you some solace and maybe even some relief. Every day is an opportunity for you to make luck happen when you harness your skills, your persistence, and your commitment to your dream.

As Casey Neistat himself has reflected, "The first 2 decades of my life were spent being told I was wrong; not fitting in. But this last decade of my life, you know those days when you're in a rush to get somewhere and you catch every green light? That's what it's felt like. I'm 33 years old, and I have no intention of slowing down."

If Albert Einstein, Francis Ford Coppola, Shane, and Casey Neistat batted leadoff through cleanup on a baseball team, they might be the best or worst hitters in the history of the major leagues. But here's the surprising truth about luck: It doesn't matter either way. As long as they keep swinging, good things are likely to happen.

Heeeeeeeeeeeey Batter, Batter, Batter, Batter! Swing, Batter!

Every time we hustle a project, be it a new company, a new product, or a new artistic vision, we go up to bat and take our best swing. Striking out is a failure. Getting on base is always good. Hitting a single is nice. A double is great. A triple is fantastic. Knocking it out of the park is sublime. And, of course, a grand slam is transcendent. Every field and industry has measures of success that can be mapped to this analogy.

In acting and filmmaking, winning an Oscar is a home run. In journalism, it's the Pulitzer Prize. In writing books, it's getting on the *New York Times* bestseller list. There are examples in any type of business: Closing a deal with a new client can be a single, double, or more—depending on the size of the deal. Getting a promotion, coveted title, and the corner office with the shiny desk is like slamming a triple. Getting a new VP job offer at that hot start-up can be a home run.

No matter how good (or bad, for that matter) we are, there is an inescapable element of luck in what sort of pitches we get to face in our careers. If you never, ever see a hanging curve, like a client with their hair on fire and six figures for you to help put it out, it is going to be tough to hit a lot of home runs. Which brings us to a dilemma: Stay at the plate or go back to the batting cages? After we have taken a couple of swings, after a few base hits and some strikeouts, we realize we have a dilemma. Given that our lives are finite, how do we optimize our probability of success? When the pitch is thrown, should we only swing for the fences and aim for home runs? Or should we take our time—say 10,000 hours—to invest in ourselves away from the game and practice the art of batting to push our average even higher?

Swing Theory

The work of psychologist Dean Keith Simonton is incredibly helpful when thinking about our personal batting problem and the longevity of our hustle. His constant-probability-of-success model suggests that once we achieve competence in our fields, our professional batting averages are firmly fixed. All of the things that make us productive in our unique ways—our nature, nurture, and our current environment—are no longer malleable nor improvable. That means that once professional competence is reached, the most successful people are not the ones with the best batting averages; the most successful just get up to bat the most.

If you're extraordinarily special, a Jedi like Luke Skywalker, you might find this depressing. If you're an ordinary palooka, like Rocky Balboa, you know that this is great news. Let's see why.

In professional baseball, if you consistently hit .300, which means you hit the ball to get on base in 3 out of 10 times at bat, you are a great baseball player. If you hit .200 (2 hits out of 10 at bats), you are of below average quality. For instance:

PLAYER	BATTING AVERAGE	AT BATS	HITS	QUALITY OF BASEBALL PLAYER	QUALITY OF HUSTLE
Luke Skywalker	.300	1,000	300	Great	Average
Rocky Balboa	.200	1,000	200	Below Average	Average

Simonton's research suggests that it's very difficult for a player to do anything about their batting average once they reach a certain level. If Rocky and Luke both wait around for perfect pitches and swing only at those, then Rocky will always have fewer hits.

But step back from the statistics and think for a minute: What matters most when it comes to who wins the game? It's not about who has the best batting average, it's who has the most hits.

Rocky's dilemma about how to become a better player is a false dichotomy: He should stop waiting for the perfect pitch and stop worrying about improving his batting average. If Rocky just gets up to bat more often, suddenly his actual impact on the game looks different.

PLAYER	BATTING AVERAGE	AT BATS	HITS	QUALITY OF BASEBALL PLAYER	QUALITY OF HUSTLE
Luke Skywalker	.300	1,000	300	Who cares?	Average
Rocky Balboa	.200	2,000	400	Who cares?	Great

Simonton's work is so exciting for hustlers because it emphasizes that we shouldn't agonize about whether we hit a single or strike out during the next at bat—we should just concentrate on getting up to bat. It doesn't matter if swinging more means missing more; doing the wrong thing (falling in love with the wrong type of person, taking a job for the wrong reasons, trying to become someone you are incapable of becoming) is amazingly helpful because it will be a wonderful assist in telling you what that right thing is.

And the best news is that life isn't like baseball—you don't have to wait your turn, you can take as many at bats as you like.

You will strike out. We all do. But remember, avoiding failure isn't the goal. And unlike in baseball, you get to stay in the game and take another turn at bat. If you're Luke, you may want to start looking over your shoulder; Rocky is coming for you.

Yet the question remains, how does Rocky discover his next at-bat? Could it be that he sees things we don't?

6

THE THREE UNSEEN LAWS OF HUSTLE

"Vision is the art of seeing what is invisible to others."

—Jonathan Swift

In *The Little Prince*, Antoine de Saint-Exupéry tells the story of a pilot who has crashed his plane in the Sahara. Shortly after his crash, he is awakened by another stranded being, a golden prince from the Asteroid B-612. The Little Prince and the nameless pilot become soul mates as they learn about each other over the course of eight bittersweet days.

The Little Prince tells the pilot about his home, about the denizens of asteroids nearby, and about what he has learned thus far on Earth—including incidents involving a snake, a fox, and a rose garden—and lest we forget, he tells the pilot of a special rose encased in protective glass still back on Asteroid B-612. The Little Prince tells the pilot that this beautiful and vain rose vexes him in his efforts to love and tend to it. His uncertainty about his relationship with the rose grows when he encounters a garden on Earth with 5,000 beautiful roses.

In one of his encounters on Earth, the Little Prince laments to a pretty fox he has just met that his rose had told him that she was unique, yet he had just seen 5,000 equally beautiful roses in a rose garden.

The sympathetic fox asks the Little Prince to tame him so they may become friends: "For you I'm only a fox like a hundred thousand other foxes. But if you tame me, we'll need each other. You'll be the only boy in the world for me. I'll be the only fox in the world for you."

After taming the fox, the Little Prince understands why his rose is unlike the other 5,000 roses. His rose is truly singular because he has tamed it, and as such it belongs to him and he belongs to it.

Before the Little Prince takes his leave of the fox, the fox imparts a final secret: "One sees clearly only with the heart. Anything essential is invisible to the eyes."

The First Unseen Law of Hustle: Do Something That *Moves* You

To slow down and begin to reverse your personal Cycle of Suck and vanquish the Mediocrity of Meh, you must momentarily forget about what is in your head. Suspend your doubts and skepticism and *look to your heart* to do something that moves you. It's easy to fall into the pattern of overthinking, and that is why you have little choice but to choose a path with your heart.

How? Do something that *moves you emotionally and moves you to take action.*

Your motivating emotion, that which feeds your hustle, need not be noble or derived from a purely positive feeling. It could just as easily come by way of a negative stirring inside you.

Perhaps it's your sense of social injustice about childhood hunger, homelessness, or pervasive mental health issues like depression that moves you to start a nonprofit organization and help others?

Perhaps it's anger at an untended problem in the marketplace—a better way to coil your iPhone earbuds so they're not a tangled mess

30 seconds before you have that all-important conference call with your boss or client—that has you launching a new product or service?

Perhaps it's sadness or frustration when thinking about the prevalence of poor child-rearing practices and your desire to democratize parental wisdom and success tips into a tool kit, thus making the toughest job in the world—raising children—easier for new parents?

Perhaps pride and vanity in a world doing all it can to ignore your talents—and your need for validation—has you putting your work into an online gallery and blog about culture that only you can control?

Maybe it's even greed. You feel deprived or excited and have a deep desire to grow your wealth and use it to buy yourself a dream home on the ocean, and one for your mom, too?

It could be revenge for that painful job rejection or a prickly unrequited love, or the desire to show a childhood bully comeuppance?

You may not be able to articulate it—and in fact, the majority of us are mostly incapable of expressing with any sort of fidelity what it is, exactly, that motivates and moves us. Our minds are designed to spend considerable effort hiding our true motivations from ourselves (as the billions of dollars spent annually on psychotherapy and psychiatric pharmaceuticals can attest).

The secret to getting moving is that, unless your motivation is explicitly rooted in hurting others, it doesn't really matter what motivates your first steps. That motivation just has to be rooted deep in yourself.

And whatever that emotion is, it needs you to tie it to your first steps. Remember what the fox said to the Little Prince: "One sees clearly only with the heart. Anything essential is invisible to the eyes."

We often end up feeling trapped in a Mediocrity of Meh because we make decisions based purely on logic and safe bets rather than listening to our hearts to find out what is essential to us.

We make the deal we shouldn't. We accept less than we should. We avoid the relationship we really want to pursue.

We may be in touch with our feelings—that is, we feel them—

but we don't bother to listen to what they're really saying to us. Like ostriches with their heads in the sand, we ignore the instincts screaming at us to avoid taking that job ("DON'T DO IT!"). And then we feel defeated when, 6 months on the job, we're feeling even more meh than ever.

Start with What, Finish with Why

Incalculable amounts of digital pixels have been rendered encouraging those of us who are stuck to "find our why"—whether in bestselling books, TED talks, or even speeches in high school gyms.

These motivators tell us that finding one's why is the first step and, therefore, the keystone to charting a life trajectory that will be both meaningful and full of money.

It's hard to think of a bigger lie than this.

Most of us, precisely 99.99997242421164824 percent of us, in fact, have no idea why we do the things we do.

Nor will we ever know, no matter how many spiritual breathing exercises, inner monologues, hippie-dippie workshops, or multiple-choice tests we indulge in.

Our "why" is a moving target, one that constantly evolves. Finding it *isn't* central to taking a first step. What is central to taking a first step . . . is taking a first step.

Our why won't ever pop fully formed out of our minds. It emerges over time and maps to our talent and our hustle.

This might strike you as counterintuitive, but your sense of a crystal clear, mission-oriented why is *not* required. Trust us, you will know a deeper why as you move through the process from momentum to meaning. Clarity comes later in your hustle, and only by virtue of your *doing*. Right now, you need to get moving, pay some bills, and sustain your physical frame. In the process, keep doing small acts that help support others in their quest to move forward. Even if it's a simple acknowledgment or social conversation, your support can offer profound benefits that lead to world-changing impact.

Never Follow Your Passion

Now, before you drop everything to launch the ceramic painting business that you've been fantasizing about since you painted your first clown, don't misinterpret our advice as simplistic *rah-rah!* tantamount to "Follow Your Passion." Following one's passion has produced more cynical, angry, tortured souls around the world than learning that Santa isn't real.*

Love to carve a wave on a surfboard? Let us guess, you want to open a surf shop?

Your cupcakes are bedazzled bombs of buttercream, and you're thinking about opening a homey, neighborhood corner bakery?

This may read as obvious, but running a retail concern like a surf shop or a bakery takes a different set of talents—accounting, inventory, marketing, customer service, for example—than charging big lefts at Brooks Street in Laguna Beach or concocting a scrumptious crumpet recipe. If running a business were so simple, we wouldn't see so many shops and restaurants serving as de facto prisons for their passion-driven owners.

You likely have all sorts of varied interests. You like football, you like reading philosophy, and you're really passionate about mathematics. So your passion drives you to pursue a career as an investment banking analyst—after all, deriving companies' valuations is a mathematical exercise. Moreover, your spreadsheet skills are sublime since you've been tracking stocks on your mom's PC since you were 11.

But when you get the job you're seeking, after the initial euphoria, a sense of malaise starts creeping in.

Something's not quite right.

Yes, you're poring over spreadsheets day and night, making sure the sophisticated models you built reference the correct cells so that your financial waterfall flows as it should, but if you're honest with yourself, you're more meh than yeah.

Why? What has your so-called passion wrought?

---

* Santa isn't real. The Easter Bunny, however, totally is.

Work in Progress in the Mirror of Experience

Typically, the strategy of following your passion suffers from a major flaw.

Your passions right now—today, as you read this book—will change considerably in the near future, the middle future, and certainly throughout your lifetime.

We hesitantly accept and know this, but, paradoxically, we don't behave like we know it. This leads to a number of hindrances in hustling successfully.

Harvard psychologist Dan Gilbert calls this the "end of history illusion." He posits that individuals across all age groups believe that they have grown and changed as much as they ever will at any given moment, and they don't sense that they will change their preferences, their loves, and their passions considerably in the future. At this moment in time and forever forward, to quote a famous sailorman-philosopher, "I yam what I yam." That is, they have reached the end of their personal history.

But our habits and, subsequently, our identities invariably do end up changing*—whether we like it or not. While this applies to everyone, anyone who has ever been married and/or had children will at some point in their life find themselves looking in the mirror and not recognizing the person staring back at them. An unfamiliar identity is a product of new habits. And with that shift in habits comes a shift in passions. In fact, our so-called passions are surprisingly ephemeral. Remember how much you loved Rick Astley in 1987? How about Chumbawamba in 1997?

So, it doesn't make much sense to let something as fleeting as a passion dictate something as important as your career. Your passion for mathematics may have gotten you the high-paying investment banking gig, but that passion is just as likely to abandon you as you evolve.

What doesn't appear to change all that much are your innate

---

* Nothing is constant but change itself" is an annoying cliché that is consistently true.

talents. The catch is, you need to do stuff—stuff that moves you—to really discover those talents.

And when you see the product of your talents, it is imperative that you invest in and double down on your strengths rather than wasting time on improving your weaknesses.

If you're midcareer and you're stuck, that likely means your strengths aren't appreciated, either by yourself or by your colleagues. Or both. Midcareer folks have a host of responsibilities that young people don't have: spouses, children, mortgages, car payments, private-preschool tuition.

This means that your hustle has to be undertaken in a measured manner. Remember, subtle not seismic shifts are the key to reversing the Cycle of Suck. You need to take baby steps down the stairs rather than sprint. History is full of late bloomers like Julia Child, no spring chicken, who first learned to cook at age 36, and then became a TV chef and icon in her fifties or Dietrich Mateschitz, the founder of Red Bull, who started his company at age 43 and became a billionaire at age 59—both of whom discovered and developed their talents at an advanced age and went on to epic accomplishments.

The landlords will tell you, "It's too late! You missed your calling." Remember to ignore them.

Because who cares? You bloomed. They didn't. As Patrick's high school Spanish teacher reminded him every morning when he slid into his seat 5 minutes late: "Más vale tarde que nunca." Better late than never.

In fact, if you're in the late stages of your career, it is just as critical that you find meaning by doing important work and being appreciated. While corporate leaders often deny ageism in hiring and firing, our anecdata show different. When you get canned 4 years before retirement because your job was outsourced, where will you and your talents be truly needed? What will move you?

The Titanic Mistake: Not Knowing the Liquid Terrain

When undertaking a hustle and exploiting an opportunity, it is critical to think about your strategy and tactics the same way the captain of an oceangoing ship thinks about navigation.

To get started, you need to familiarize yourself with all of the obvious hazards and easily observed phenomena above the surface. As a captain, you keep navigation charts and tools at hand just for this purpose: knowing the liquid terrain. In what direction is the wind blowing? How fast? What is the temperature of the air? What is the temperature of the water? Are there high waves or is the sea choppy? Are there supertankers on your course? When does the sun rise, and when does the sun set?

Are there any pirates in the area? Any icebergs? Hello, *Titanic*!

There are similar hazards and phenomena in any job. For example, if you want to get promoted with a raise, you need to understand how the company finances are doing. How about revenues last quarter? Where did the company fail to execute well? What drove growth?

And that's where most people stop. They check and recheck their maps, and they observe and record the most easily available, most visible information. And then they act on it. That's when they steam directly into an iceberg.

The especially wily captains and seasoned hustlers, on the other hand, make sure to understand what's below the surface, too: reefs, wrecks, and buried treasure.

The Seen Unseen

Unseen obstructions and undercurrents often determine most of what is happening on the surface. The waves that surfers ride are created by moving water hitting a slab of rock 20 feet under the surface. You only know to ride the wave if you know where that slab of rock is when the hurricane swell comes.

Unseen undercurrents are there to be tapped into. When you are at the beach and you swim out from shore a bit and an unseen force grabs you and pulls you out, don't panic and try to swim straight back to shore. You'll just tire out. Let the water take you out and then swim parallel to shore for a bit. Sure, it'll feel like it takes a bit longer, but you're going with the flow, not fighting it. For example, if you're negotiating a deal and you feel the other party behaving in an irrational manner, trying to steer you strongly in one direction, suss out the unspoken motivation that's really driving this behavior, and then take advantage of it. Don't use hyperlogic and try to persuade them of their wrongheaded approach.

Undercurrents Redraw Maps

Undercurrents constantly shift sands and erase and remake reefs, making navigation maps less than useful in stormy water. What worked yesterday might not work tomorrow. And the buried treasure that everyone forgot about may have just been uncovered by last year's storm. The received wisdom about how to do something may be accurate for a while, but knowledge has an expiration date. That brings us to the Second Unseen Law of Hustle.

The Second Unseen Law of Hustle: Keep Your Head Up and Your Eyes Open

When you keep your head up and your eyes open, you see and seize opportunity where most do not. By *seeing the unseen* and identifying unexploited opportunity, you are led only to more momentum and, inevitably, to the outcomes that sustain your money, meaning, and momentum.

Currents Are Faster Than the Wind

In a 1785 letter concerning oceanic trade and seafaring vessels, legendary polymath Benjamin Franklin noted, "Vessels are sometimes retarded, and sometimes forwarded in their voyages, by currents at sea, which are often not perceived."

Aside from being a founding father, diplomat, and inventor, Franklin was also an explorer of the unseen. In his many voyages from the American colonies to England and back, Franklin noticed an interesting phenomenon: At some point during his travel, the color of the Atlantic Ocean would change, the ship would experience what he characterized as "hot damp winds," and seaweed would be clearly seen on the water's surface. Franklin thought this meant that the ship was near the coast, but he was disabused of this notion by the ship's captain, who was adamant that they were still far from land.

Ponce de León and his men had come across the same phenomenon more than 200 years earlier, namely that a virtual "river in the ocean" exists and at its fastest current of roughly 6 miles per hour is about 300 times faster than the slow flow of the Amazon River. This current allowed ships sailing from the American colonies to England to make the trip 2 weeks faster than those going in the opposite direction.

Franklin had rediscovered and charted what we now know as the Gulf Stream. The Gulf Stream is a set of warm water currents traveling counterclockwise up North America's Atlantic Coast, east across the North Atlantic, and then south to northwestern Europe. If you are sailing from west to east, you'd be advantaged to sail in its flow. If you are sailing from east to west, you'd best avoid it, as it will slow you down.

The Gulf Stream takes ships in an indirect path across the Atlantic, but it's an optimal one in terms of speed. Sailors crossing from the American colonies to England along the Gulf Stream took a geographically longer route but ended up at their destination faster than if they had sailed in a straight line due east from point A to point B.

The Second Unseen Law of Hustle demands that hustlers tap into undercurrents to see and get stuff done faster.

Drawing on a Different Side of Hustle

Not too long ago, Jonas asked his friend Josh, an accomplished illustrator and artist, the best way to begin improving his sketching and drawing skills.

"Ah. That's a good question," replied Josh. "You might think that it's about constantly practicing your fine motor skills by drawing perfect circles and straight lines. And if you did, you'd be forgiven for thinking so. Most beginning artists mistake the craft of drawing with the physical movement of the artist's hands. While those fine motor skills are important, what they're missing is that before you draw, you have to learn to see like an artist sees the world. Once you learn to see and *un*see, the world reveals itself to you. My hands moving across paper are the output, not the input."

Josh went on to explain that when we look at faces, our minds instantly ascribe meaning and context to them. That is, when we see a face, we know if the person we are looking at is happy, sad, or angry, which makes drawing, say, a wrinkle on a smiling person's face incredibly hard. We emotionally feel and see the smile; we don't see the shape of the light and shadow and how they interact with the muscles of the mouth and eyes to create a smile. This is why introductory drawing classes often have students copy pictures of upside-down faces. When you look at a face upside down, you see it more objectively because you have tricked your mind from blinding you with its context interpretation.

And so it is with hustling. Before you can hustle, you must learn to see differently.

Where most others see dangerous obstacles in their path, hustlers are like practitioners of parkour, viewing walls as springboards and obstacles as playgrounds. Where most people see fear and pain, hustlers see opportunity—oceans of it.

Oceans of Opportunity

Okay, great, so you're in. Now what does opportunity look like, where does it reside, and how will we recognize it when it jumps out of the sea, lands at our feet, and flops around madly on our deck? Opportunity abounds in every conversation or interaction you find yourself in. It may not be apparent on the surface, but trust that it's there in more ways than you can imagine.

Paradoxically, most of the time we already know what to do to set our heart in motion, keep our head up, and hustle our way to success. We know exactly how to connect B (outcome) to A (initiation point)— yet something stops us from taking action.

As we set out on our hustle, the little voice in our head tells us, "It cannot be that easy. If it were, other people would be doing it."

There it is. You've done it, with that seemingly innocuous thought, you are now officially stuck.

You're in good company, though. No less august an entity than the British Post Office refused to listen to Ben Franklin's advice about the existence of the Gulf Stream. In the late-18th century, they refused to harvest an opportunity that would have cut 2 weeks from the time it took for their ships to voyage east across the Atlantic, saving lives and money.

Let us unstick you.

Ask yourself, Is what you're trying to do easy or simple? Here's a clue: They're not the same.

Most of the time, people use the word *easy* to describe a situation that is actually *simple*. When something is simple, the situation has relatively few moving parts and can be easily understood by a newcomer. But something simple can still be hard.

Recognizing Opportunity: The Hustle Sweet Spot

To identify the hustler's sweet spot, we've broken down the world of projects into four categories.

Simple to Understand, Easy to Do: Start a blog, respond to a job posting. Houston, we have a problem. Everyone can do these—there's little risk and limited reward.

Complicated to Understand, Easy to Do: Learn how to play poker like a professional, code a gaming app, fly an airplane. These are complex tasks with lots of moving parts, at least initially, and most people do not survive the early learning curve.

Complicated to Understand, Hard to Do: Learn to perform cardiac surgery, develop a lightning-fast electric car. There's little room for error, and most will avoid tasks in this quadrant. They are too complex and have too many moving parts.

Simple to Understand, Hard to Do: Write a book, launch a successful start-up, close new business, get a job promotion. This is the Hustle Sweet Spot because you win by blocking the naysayers and charging ahead while absorbing small doses of pain.

Deadlines Are Lifelines

Ira Glass, American radio personality and host of the wildly popular radio show *This American Life,* once advised anyone seeking a career in creative work: "Most everybody I know who does interesting, creative work went through a phase of years of where they could tell what they were making wasn't as good as they wanted it to be. We know our work doesn't have this special thing that we want it to have. We all go through this. And if you are just starting out or you are still in this phase, you gotta know it's normal and the most important thing you can do is do a lot of work. Put yourself on a deadline so that every week you will finish one story. It is only by going through a volume of work that you will close that gap, and your work will be as good as your ambitions."

Put yourself on a deadline. Focus on volume and completion.

To maintain momentum, we need closure. Many people build momentum following the first two Unseen Laws of Hustle, and once they approach the third law, things begin to peter out.

The Third, Last, and Possibly Scariest Law of All: Seal the Deal and Make It Real

This law demands a transaction. It demands proof of your hustle. No more talk. Put up or shut up.

This is when we close the gap between what we said we would do and what we have done. Without this step, we end up not hustling but spinning in our hamster wheel indefinitely, a waste of energy without a goal. We've all tried this at one point in our lives, and the ending is always the same. Extreme fatigue and a crisis of meaning.

The Third Unseen Law of Hustle is the temporary closure we all need. It gives us a moment to ring the bell, punctuate our wins, take a deep breath, reorient with what we've learned, and start anew. Sealing the deal doesn't have to be in the form of a massive seven-figure check. But it does have to be a concrete commitment.

Want to write a book?

Set your alarm for 4:30 a.m. and write until 8:00 a.m. Do this for one week. Show your 10,000-word rough draft to a friend. You've just sealed the deal and made it real.

Want to start your own company?

Forget filing the incorporation docs. Forget the fancy-schmancy logo.

Sell something to a brand-new customer. "Get them to sign on the line which is dotted." Seal the deal and make it real.

Aside from making it real for you and giving you confidence in your growing abilities, sealing the deal makes it real for your friends, your family, and your colleagues. It prepares them for the forthcoming transformation. Anyone who witnesses milestones of your hustle will gladly help you as your habits and identities shift.

Betray Yourself to Stay True to Yourself

Today, Ursula Burns serves as chairman and chief executive officer of Xerox. She is the first African American woman to become a CEO of a Fortune 500 company. Yesterday, raised by her mother in the projects of the Lower East Side of Manhattan, she appeared to have several strikes against her.

Strike one: She was black.

Strike two: She was female.

Strike three: She was poor.

Society sez, "Thanks for playing, Ursula. You're OUT!"*

---

* As Ursula proves, African American women are just as capable as any other humans. However, society's unfair perceptions can indeed hinder our hustle.

Ursula's mother worked incalculably hard to ensure that her daughter had a strong education at strict Catholic schools, but in our view, more important than that was the belief that Ursula's mom instilled in her. "She constantly reminded me that where I was didn't define who I was," Ursula remembered.

Whether triggered by your own discomfort with change ("I cannot become successful because I have never been successful.") or by your well-meaning friends ("She cannot be a CEO because she doesn't have the experience to be a CEO. I am only trying to save her from failure."), one of the greatest traps you can find yourself in is, in Emerson's words, maintaining a "foolish consistency" between your past self and your present self.

As you seal the deal and make it real, your habits will inevitably be forced to change. And when habits change, new identities are formed. Never forget: Habits create identities, identities don't create habits.

> Do I contradict myself?
>
> Very well then I contradict myself,
>
> (I am large, I contain multitudes.)
>
> —Walt Whitman, "Song of Myself"

Our identities—who we were and who we will be—are neither fixed nor consistent with one another (nor should they be!) as Dan Gilbert's research reminds us.

Yesterday's you isn't the same as today's you. Tomorrow's you looks even more impressive.

In the past, the saying used to be "Dress for the job you want, not the job you have." But in a world where CEOs wear T-shirts and jeans to work, the new model needs to be "Think for the life you want, not the life you have."

To be loyal to our personal hustle, we must willingly betray our old self so that our new self gains momentum.

Art Imitates Life

The year is 1975. A late-twenties, down-on-his-luck actor is desperate, hungry, broke, and has just sold his dog, along with his wife's jewelry, to pay the bills. He has hit a low point in his life and can't land any roles. One night he stumbles on a televised boxing match between the champ, Muhammad Ali, and some no-name palooka named Chuck Wepner.

During the fight, Wepner not only knocks down Ali, the best fighter in the world, but he damn near beats him. Ali goes on to win in a controversial stoppage in the final round of the fight, but seeing Wepner's courage, his will to win, and his effort to leave nothing on the table left an indelible mark on the young actor, a spark of inspiration that transformed him from nobody to legend. The excited actor loads up on caffeine and works through the night, hammering away on his old typewriter. And boom, Rocky Balboa is born. The actor, Sylvester Stallone, sends the script around Hollywood, and the offers start rolling in: $50,000, $100,000, eventually topping out at $300,000—more than $1 million in today's money. Even though he's broke and battered, Stallone passes on the big money.

Stallone insists that producers allow him to write *and* act in the movie. He insists that he must play the starring role or there's no deal. And guess what? Eventually, he wins, gets some money for the script, and keeps the role of Rocky for himself. The movie is shot on a shoe-string budget, and a year or so later, the film blows up. It earns him and the production a handsome return on their investment, along with multiple Academy Award nominations, including ones for Best Original Screenplay and Best Actor. The film ultimately wins the Oscar for Best Picture.

(We want to highlight that Stallone literally rewrote his identity by writing *Rocky*. And Rocky Balboa, the character he created, follows suit, transforming from debt collector to heavyweight contender.)

What lessons can we extract from the story?

Never give up?

Believe in yourself?

Be bold?

Trust your instincts?

Nope.

Nah.

Nein.

No.

These sorts of commonly held misconceptions that have been perpetuated for millennia don't help us own our dreams.

The truth has nothing to do with 10,000 hours or grinding it out; the hidden truth is in always keeping the wheels turning, because *momentum*—the willful act of doing—is our secret weapon, our equalizer. Always has been, always will be.

Just by reading this chapter, your brain has already started rewiring itself. You are well on your way to internalizing the Three Unseen Laws of Hustle. We promise they will change the way you think—the way you do.

You are now seeing with your heart, your eyes are trained on activity below the surface, and you are well on your way to establishing action-oriented habits that keep you moving. The natural consequences of these changes will have you following a different, indirect path to success.

7

YOUR INDIRECT PATH: UNIQUE AND OBLIQUE

"The straight line is ungodly."

—Friedensreich Hundertwasser

Too often we blindly assume that the shortest distance between two points is a straight line, direct—a point A to point B experience. We've been led astray by society's conventional thinking, and we've accepted this to be the most accurate truth.

But it's a lie.

Obliquity: The Point B to Point A Play

When NASA launched MESSENGER, a robotic spacecraft that was to orbit and study the planet Mercury, in August 2004, they didn't elect to launch it with an intergalactic sniper's shot of 48 million miles in a straight line from Earth to Mercury.

Sending MESSENGER in a straight line to Mercury would have been too risky—the sun's gravity field would have accelerated it too far, too fast, making its speed too great to achieve a permanent orbit around Mercury, from where it could survey Mercurial gravity fields and geography. To decelerate MESSENGER would have required that the craft carry a significant volume of heavy fuel, which would have made the actual launch from Earth untenable.

To help solve the issue, NASA dusted off a 1985 study that proposed an unconventional approach that might offer a successful solution to this catch-22. The proposal suggested that multiple gravity assists, by which a spacecraft harnesses a planet's gravity field by executing "flybys," could be used to both speed up and slow down the spacecraft with minimal fuel requirements.

The recharted trajectory sent MESSENGER on multiple flybys with Earth, Venus, and Mercury—amounting to a journey of 4.9 billion miles, lasting 6 years, 7 months, and 16 days before a wildly successful insertion into Mercury's orbit.

If you're keeping track, the method from 1985 was 100 times longer in distance than the sniper's shot, but it's the method that had a chance to succeed. This, ladies and gentlemen, is obliquity: the principle that the fastest, clearest, and most legible path isn't always the one that will get you where you actually want to go.

Obliquely Dreaming

When it comes to obliquity and your dreams, here's how it works: Far too many of us set our sights on a dream and then grind it out trying to put together the resources, skills, network, and opportunities in a sequence prescribed by conventional wisdom that might make that dream possible.

That's what we call the point A to point B route.

The indisputable problem with that approach is "nobody knows anything."* The collective conventional wisdom doesn't know you,

---

* The quote comes from William Goldman's book *Adventures in the Screen Trade*. The entire quote is "Nobody knows anything. Not one person in the entire motion picture field knows for a certainty what's going to work. Every time out it's a guess and, if you're lucky, an educated one." This applies to every industry known to man.

doesn't know who you are, doesn't know what you're good or bad at—and it certainly doesn't know why you do what you do.

If Neil had listened to the conventional wisdom as a young college student, he'd probably be a doctor, neck-deep in student loans and stuck in a Cycle of Suck. Neil would likely have been a decent doctor—decent but miserable—and his hidden talents as a digital marketer would likely have lain fallow. But these very same talents are what allow him to flourish professionally and personally.

Jonas was expected, in his words, to be a "good Jewish boy": doctor, lawyer, professor, or GTFO. The pressure was strong from his family—not because they didn't love him, but because they did love him and wanted the best for him. Luckily, he listened to his gut, brushed aside the limitations of conventional thinking, and manufactured an exciting and creative career consulting, writing, and working with people and projects he truly enjoys.

Patrick tried his best to listen to the conventional wisdom, and in a career effort of keeping up with the Joneses, he scrapped for stints at consultancies and investment banks, each time getting mauled in no-win environments that marginalized his unique strengths and magnified his weaknesses. He estimates that he wasted most of his twenties looking into the fun house mirrors for guidance on career choice and path. As he is wont to say about those years: FML.

What if instead of listening to conventional wisdom, you take a look at yourself in the mirror of experience. This completely honest look at yourself will evaluate the talents inside you and then allow them to guide you on your journey?

You do you.

This is what we call the point B to point A route: You look at the resources—paramount, your unique talents—available to you and use them to take you in whatever wonderful, unexpected, unpredictable direction you choose. This will, at times, be the longer path, and it may certainly be the least direct, but it is the path that allows you to devote all of your resources and energy toward actively owning your dream.

Hustle and Obliquity

In his enchanting little book *Obliquity*, economist John Kay says that the best way to achieve complex goals is through "oblique," that is, indirect, means.

In the introduction to this book, we defined hustle as an indirect yet decisive movement toward a goal, by which the motion itself manufactures luck, surfaces hidden opportunities, and builds more money, meaning, and momentum in our lives.

When you take an oblique step, the path itself responds by opening to you in a way you didn't see beforehand, which begets another step. And another. You might not realize in the moment where each step is taking you, but the act of stepping creates opportunities and luck that would not have existed otherwise.

The poet Muriel Strode once wrote, "Do not follow where the path may lead. Go instead where there is no path and leave a trail."

The reason hustle and obliquity are so well matched is that while hustle has you finding your own gifts, obliquity has you putting them to use in unique ways.

The Pull of Hustle

If you think about it, your hustle needs to lead; it pulls you—not pushes you—off the beaten path and down an original path that is wholly yours and designed by you.

This is essentially the difference between a father standing on the pool deck haranguing his 3-year-old daughter to jump in the deep end already and the same father standing in the water beckoning her to join him. The first scenario is fraught with fear; the latter is an exciting and fun adventure.

Indirect Ascents and Unexpected Destinations

Some years back, Jonas and a couple of friends traveled by train through Europe. They stopped for a few days in picturesque Interlaken,

Switzerland, to take in the scenery of this small town inhabited by quiet, well-mannered residents and take on a new challenge: finding the best local beer and the most grueling hike possible.

Seemingly suspended in time, Interlaken is a haltingly beautiful landscape. There, in the Swiss Alps, snowcapped mountains explode upward like watchful elders hovering protectively, and dense green slopes descend down to the valley below. Majestic and magnificent, the mountains inspire you with a sense of awe and invite you to delight in their awesomeness. It's a place where it's impossible not to feel a curiosity about the natural scenery around you, and where most people make time to hike or walk, a national pastime in Switzerland.

A day after decompressing from their long train ride, Jonas and company followed suit. They walked around and surveyed the options, finally handpicking for their trek a long hike on the Eiger Trail to not just any mountain, but one of the highest peaks in the area, called Mönch. Towering at more than 13,000 feet above sea level, with jagged cliffs, treacherous trails, pristine pastures, and brown Swiss cows, this is as close as it gets to a real-life *Sound of Music* scenario.

After a few rounds of beer, Jonas and his friends confidently set out a plan to speedily make their way up the slope. The next morning, they began from the foothills above the town, hooked up with a few Australian hikers, and set out on what seemed like a manageable hike. It wasn't.

The trails climbed and twisted, and the more Jonas's group felt like they were making progress, the more they realized the deceptive nature of ascents. It was grueling, and making things worse, the trail they'd set out on was closed due to a dangerous rockslide.

They weighed the options. They could:

A) Bypass the trail and take another route to Mönch—a dangerous nonstarter.

B) Call it a day and return to Interlaken—unfulfilling meh.

C) Shift course and descend to reach the western end of the Eiger Trail and head to another peak, Schilthorn—

adventurous, fulfilling, and justification for more rounds
of beer.

They of course chose option C: heading backward and due west
in the direction of Schilthorn, a mountain that holds the distinction
of being featured in a number of spectacular scenes in the 1969 James
Bond film *On Her Majesty's Secret Service*. They were game.

They set out on the treacherous, exhausting, never-again, 7-hour
summit, making stops along the way. And for each insanely steep
ascent portion, and there were plenty of them, they met with turns
that *descended* into emerald green valleys and plateaus with crystal
blue lakes unlike any scenery any of them had ever seen. They were
hiking through a movie set it seemed, and with no guide and only a
vague sense of destination. And instead of a rapid up-and-over tra-
verse of the mountain rise, they met twisting zigzags and dizzying
corkscrews along the trail.

Beaten down but exhilarated, eventually they reached the peak.
From the base of the trail, they had looked up and thought, We can
do that—no big deal. But once they started out hiking and climbing,
hand over hand, they'd entered a world of pain. Sometimes you find
it's easier to go down, even when you want to go up. *And sometimes
going up means taking a different path entirely.*

This experience of movement was far from a slingshot of effi-
ciency from base to summit. Each ascent was followed by a descent or
sideways trajectory. As we climb through our lives and our work, we
notice a route that looks similar. Rarely, if ever, do we find the way
that leads straight from base to summit. And sometimes the summit
we set out to ascend is not the summit we eventually reach.

If experience teaches us anything, it's that the route we set out
on, however well planned, is illusory even in the best terrain. It tricks
us into seeing ski lifts where there are none. And, even if there were,
it's unlikely we'd have a lift ticket anyway.

Like us, you've likely looked for a shortcut or accelerator on your
path to success. Some might call this a hack. And tactically, it can be
said there's a hack for just about everything, especially in business.

But often, to discover said hack, we have to search obliquely, not on the straight and narrow slope. In the bigger picture of life, hacks frequently emerge from unexpected turns, the zigzags and rebounds, the downside of the upside. In real life, we reach point B, our destination, via a line that's anything but straight.

As you hustle in life, you're going to find a path beset by switchbacks. You'll start in one direction, and as soon as you've made headway, you'll find yourself cutting back in the opposite direction. The same point applies to work. Advancement—when we create a product, launch a service, sell a design, draw praise from our boss, put together a deal with a client, gain a promotion, or discover a new way of solving a problem—often happens indirectly. It comes about as a product of our route, not because of the path itself. Eventually, as you keep climbing, you'll make major vertical headway and reach a peak, and you'll look down in astonishment. And after reflection, you'll know you've changed.

Before you look for that next mountain, consider these lessons of the oblique ascent. You're undoubtedly making one, and it helps to be conscious of it.

Forget Their Route: It's the Wrong Way for You

These ideas about switchbacks and obliquity aren't just conveniently interesting hiccups of geography, they're also the natural terrain of successful hustlers.

When you want to climb a mountain, the shortest way is a geometric straight line up from the base to the peak—but in reality, unless Mommy and Daddy bought you a helicopter ride, a route straight up doesn't even exist.

The way you summit the mountain is by following a series of switchbacks. Sometimes they appear to take you away from the peak, and sometimes they even have you going downhill, but ultimately they are the route to the top.

What's so beautiful about obliquity is that we can tailor it to our own skills and needs. The route you might use to climb a particular mountain is likely different than ours, even though our end points are the same. As a hustler, it is critical that you *always design your own way* from point B to point A—creating a path optimized for yourself. Everyone has different talents, skills, and experiences, and that means everyone has their own best path. Try to follow somebody else and you're at the mercy of *their* skill set. You're just going to feel like they're better, faster, and smarter than you, but that's only because you're not forging the path based on *your* training and innate abilities.

Great, you say. I get it. I need to go backward to figure out how to get from point B to point A. But what if there is no easy path to reach point B?

That's the point. If Mommy and Daddy won't spring for a ride, and there is no easy way to reach point B, it's because no such path exists. You need to create the path.

There will always be people who go from point A to point B because tradition has made it so. But just because they follow the status quo shouldn't stop you from blazing your own path.

You name the industry, and you'll see a social convention exists, one that forces you on the beaten path from point A to point B. These conventions exist because they reinforce the status quo. All the gatekeepers want you to go through this process because the process favors and actually serves their interests first and yours last, if at all.

Reverse Engineering a Taxi Pickup

"There is no way we're getting in that line."

Our friend Ben gestured irritably in the direction of the taxi line—at least 200 people deep—outside the lobby of the Venetian hotel and casino in Las Vegas. The Consumer Electronics Show (CES) was in full swing, and the Venetian currently was overflowing with business-casual-clad masses proudly bearing conference badges.

Ben turned, fixed us with a stare, and with a thick Austrian accent slowly intoned, "Come with me if you want to live."

Rubbing his aching temples and remembering the one-too-many cocktails he'd had the night before, Patrick chuckled softly but not so much that his head would explode.

Ben broke into a trot, ignoring the small army of uniformed hotel porters and bellboys motioning us toward taxi line stanchions designed to corral sheeple. We headed for the middle of the roundabout teeming with taxis dropping off passengers at the hotel.

Ben waved down a sharp-eyed taxi driver whose cab had just disgorged four eager, khaki-clad CES attendees.

"Yo! Three headed to the Wynn."

"Get in quick."

We hopped in, and when one of the valets wagged his finger at us as we drove past, we started grinning like self-satisfied schoolchildren.

How to Reverse Engineer

Let's walk through the taxi scenario above, and this time let's place you in it. You have just come down from your Vegas hotel room and are looking for a taxi, and the line is 200 people long. You look to your right and see the bland sheeple considering the same line.

Step I: Are You Framing the Right Problem?

The sheeple consider the taxi line's length the problem, but you know that's not so. The actual problem doesn't change: You need a cab. But you're less attached to exactly how you get that cab as long as you get it.

Step 2: Are You Seeing Unconventional Solutions?

Instinctively, the sheeple will do what they always do—stay on the point A to point B path because it's the path of least resistance. Waiting in line is annoying, but, hey, that's what smartphones are for: to entertain us as we wait around for life to happen to us behind the stanchions. Right. Uh, right, guys? You determine you have a few choices.

A) You could wait in line. Meh.

B) You could maybe go back up to your room and call a cab. Not much better, but at least your habit for hustle has developed in you a bias for action and a healthy appetite for (small) risk.

C) With those in hand, you quite literally see other possible unconventional solutions that remain completely unseen to the sheeple. There are empty cabs leaving the premises of the hotel 100 feet in front of you. No law demands that you stand in line or that you conform to the tacit sequence of grabbing a cab. Why not move your bod 100 feet over and jump in?

Reverse engineering outcomes—starting at point B to end at point A—is a learned skill that will serve you in life, and it works in innumerable ways. Practically everything we think of or can accomplish—whether it's a creating a new product, developing a new process, having a new experience, or even catching a cab—can be approached obliquely and be made to work to our unique benefit. It just requires a subtle reworking of the accepted rules because sequences on the way from point A to point B are mostly social convention.

In the process of hustling, we apply the sweet, sweet science of getting shit done unencumbered by social convention. Reverse engineering the sequencing means doing things in an unconventional order.

Taking Your Bank Shot to the Bank

In 2011, Dr. Larry Silverberg, an engineering professor at North Carolina State University, basketball enthusiast, and developer of sophisticated algorithms, published research exploring a question that has troubled children on driveways all over the United States since the days of James Naismith: Go for the swish or bank it in? Shoot a basket with or without the ball hitting the backboard first? Go from point A (your hand) to point B (the net) directly or use the glass?

Silverberg's computer-aided simulation strongly suggests that a large swath of the basketball half-court close to the hoop you're shooting at is much better exploited by shooting a bank shot than a direct shot. In some cases, basketball players are 20 percent more likely to score by switching to a bank shot.

According to Silverberg, this is because when a ball banks off the backboard, the physics of the shot ensure that the ball loses a significant amount of energy, which allows a less accurate angle and makes for a more forgiving hoop, as opposed to the need for absolute precision when going for nothing but net.

In basketball and in life, an oblique method pays off.

From our quest to manufacture more luck to our exploration of outer space to our quest for personal achievement, by bending the laws of conventional thinking and going from point B to point A in our oblique way, we get more results in our own bespoke fashion.

Which leads us to the question: If we can leverage the laws of physics to obliquely navigate through the deepest reaches of space as well as to better our ability to score more points in basketball here on Earth, can we not do the same to choose an adventurous path that moves us closer to more money, meaning, and momentum?

8

CHOOSE YOUR OWN ADVENTURE

"It is only in adventure that some people succeed in knowing themselves—in finding themselves."

—André Gide

Now that we have a clear sense of obliquity in mind, it's time to take a look at the big picture and your path forward. The next level of hustle is where the rubber meets the road, where your life takes on a new direction. You already know that it's your movement that matters most: the checkmate that changes life, the professional pièce de résistance that pleases your parents—and pays the bills.

The way to get ahead boils down to four kinds of hustle—four archetypes for meaningfully pushing your career and your path forward, shaking things up to show you the opportunity of what comes next. These pathways are equally imaginative, open-source shortcuts to rapid, sustained growth. When they're taken together, we view all four as parts of a fluid model for understanding your options, further developing your potential, and paving the way forward from the abyss into the bliss that is your future.

What's exciting here is that these avenues apply if you're starting your journey as a job candidate, working your way up into a management or major leadership role, or starting or growing your business—online or offline. All paths lead to making a big breakthrough happen—a new job offer, a promotion, a move to freelancing or small business, launching your own start-up, or even selling your business.

Each of the four pathways works with a high degree of predictability and repeatability. And just like with obliquity, the path forward implies movement not in a unidirectional straight line, but instead in a route that leads up, down, and sideways, ultimately pulling you from what you are to what you will become.

The Fourfold Path

1. **Outside/Inside Hustle** is getting a foot in the door.

2. **Inside/Upside Hustle** is proving your value and earning a promotion.

3. **Inside/Outside Hustle** is diving into entrepreneurial waters.

4. **Outside/Upside Hustle** is accelerating epic entrepreneurial and creative achievements.

I. The Outside/Inside Hustle

Want to get hired at the next great start-up or at a Fortune 100 or make the leap from school (or no school) to your first meaningful gig? You need the Outside/Inside Hustle. Think of it as getting a firm foot in the door—a launchpad to put you on the path toward owning your dreams. Today, an increasingly common form of this is informal apprenticeships—whereby employers take a risk on your lack of specific professional experience in exchange for helping you rapidly acquire a valuable skill set.

The key to the Outside/Inside Hustle is doing what everyone else *isn't*. Whatever you do, don't—we repeat, *don't*—just send your résumé in over e-mail. Don't wait around for an automated "Thank you for submitting your application" response from an anonymous HR e-mail address, either. There are better ways to hustle.

Instead, circumvent the gatekeeper in HR. Be willing to go around the conventions. Find out who the real decision maker is and approach them directly, or make them come to you. Ryan Graves did just that, creating the opportunity he wanted and beating out a competitive field of applicants—some with more experience, more connections, more expertise, and more pedigree—to land a dream job at a start-up.

After acknowledging his Mediocrity of Meh and the limitations of a nine-to-five, dead-end job as a database administrator at a huge multinational conglomerate, Ryan got radical. He saw the Foursquare app as the grail: an innovative start-up with big potential. Feeling trapped on the outside, he wanted to be in the start-up world . . . bad.

Ryan had applied—and gotten turned down—for a position at Foursquare in the past. Even still, he felt undeterred. He knew his way in, and that way was the Outside/Inside Hustle. The way Foursquare works is it connects individuals with businesses that they're geographically close to. Ryan saw an opportunity to work for the company, even though he didn't "work" "for" "the company."

Here's Ryan's genius angle: He spent time calling bars in Chicago, pitching and selling their staff on the benefits of Foursquare, teaching the staff how to use the app, and gathering support and sign-ups. It was small doses of pain, an experimental side project he felt confident taking some swings at. Since he'd already been turned down for the job, the risks were limited. The Outside/Inside Hustle would only make him stronger.

Ryan, still desperate to get away from his role at the stodgy multinational, put in overtime during his "off-time," working for Foursquare even though he didn't technically have a job there. He signed up a bunch of businesses and—get this—he e-mailed the list of these new customers to people and investors affiliated with Foursquare. And guess what happened? Foursquare told him to keep doing what he was doing—business development—and they made him an offer he couldn't refuse. He was now a Foursquare employee with a paycheck and stock options. Why? Because he did the unexpected and found a way to leverage his luck in a way that other applicants had overlooked.

Today, Ryan continues to make waves at a little company called Uber. Oh, and he's a billionaire. All this because of his fondness for an app, willingness to experiment, and refusal to let go of his dream. That's the Outside/Inside Hustle.

Jonas found luck—with his own Outside/Inside Hustle—beating out a competitive field of applicants, some with an additional 20 years of experience, to land a dream job as a billionaire's apprentice.

Jonas Moves from the Outside to the Inside

If you want to work on your pitching, it never hurts to find out who is the real hiring decision maker for any job or new business deal and approach them directly.

After discovering a mysterious job listing—"Join a *NY Times* best-selling writing team—work with the chairman of the board"—Jonas, instead of first preparing his résumé and going through the normal application process, picked up the phone and called the company directly. He didn't stop at the receptionist or the nondecision makers. He went straight to the top, got on the phone with the executive's assistant, asked specific questions about the job opportunity, and developed a rapport with the executive's team *before* he submitted his credentials for review. He *differentiated himself* from the rest of the pack to set the stage for the opportunity of a lifetime—one that put him at the table with real estate icons who were revolutionizing an industry. This gave Jonas an instant dose of hormesis and, when he eventually got hired, a multiyear, life-changing boost of momentum, money, and meaning that propelled him forward in unforeseen ways.

All this started with one phone call, and with trusting the Outside/Inside Hustle. It works.

2. The Inside/Upside Hustle

You're coasting along on a path that you're happy with, but you're also hungry for the opportunity to build more momentum, make more money, and have more meaning in your life. Guess what? You're ready for the Inside/Upside Hustle, a pathway best described as an ascent, one characterized by growth and new challenges *within* an organization. The key here is that the organization you choose to commit to must be one whose values and vision align with your own. If the organization you're in doesn't map to where you see yourself growing or doesn't present opportunities for growth, then this is not the optimal pathway for you. If, on the other hand, you are with a company that already rewards you and you wish to grow with it for a long time, then this hustle is well worth the pursuit.

The key difference with the Inside/Upside Hustle is that you're *already established* in a regular work situation, and you have a firm existing role in a company. You have a title and defined responsibilities, work that gives you stimulating challenges and an ability to contribute meaningfully—and, even more, you have clarity about the direction of the company's future because leadership transparency indicates the company is on an excellent trajectory. You also need a positive working relationship with your manager and the respect of your peers.

Think about the project manager who's been a rock of reliability on the team for 2 years: She has a desire to take on more responsibility and manage more of the company. Or the analyst on a team at an investment bank: She reviews a list of companies within an industry yet wants to make her future in forging higher-level M&A partnerships for those companies. Or the junior copywriter on a large advertising account who wants to become the next Don Draper. In a civic role, it could be the middle school teacher who wants to become that school's administrator or principal. It could even be the ambitious mailroom grunt at a talent agency with his eyes on becoming the next Hollywood mogul.

In the Inside/Upside Hustle, your job looks ostensibly secure and you're ready for something more. This was certainly the case for introvert Hugh Forrest. Meeting him, one might perceive an ambition more subtle than in your face. But dig a bit deeper and you see this specimen of Quirky Luck and soft-spoken steadiness as something else entirely.

In 1987, while working as a contributor to the *Austin Chronicle*, a community and arts alt-weekly in Austin, Texas, Hugh got an offer from the paper's founders to help out with their seedling music festival start-up, South by Southwest. Yes, *that* SXSW.

Hugh was officially SXSW's first paid nonvolunteer, employee number 1. Though not a techie, Hugh was nonetheless hired to handle the festival's technology and desktop-publishing needs, which made sense, since he was the only person in the organization who had an "expensive computer." Hugh helped the founders by wearing many hats—writing, planning, content programming, marketing, designing, taking phone calls, and doing whatever else was required.

What drew Hugh in was the flexible culture established by the founders and the chance to be a part of something fun and innovative that might one day become a great music festival. Intrigued by the opportunity to shape the attendee experience as well as hear great bands, Hugh and SXSW's team of volunteers worked hard. The fledgling festival immediately found an audience of music fans—and music would be the only SXSW cash cow in the early years. More people—industry reps, unknown acts looking to get discovered, and music enthusiasts from around the globe—began flocking south in March for a break from the cold weather.

While the festival was growing, Hugh hit a wall, and before fully committing his professional career to the festival, he decided on a temporary detour. He briefly left SXSW to try his hand at a newly launched music magazine. It didn't turn out to be nearly as exciting as the festival, nor as promising. Hugh's belief in the festival, friendships with the founders, and sense of a unique growth opportunity soon brought him back to SXSW. He immediately picked up where he had left off, and this time with the promotion to festival director.

Hugh-ing to the Second Unseen Law of Hustle (Keep Your Head Up and Your Eyes Open), by 1994, Hugh noticed that many music acts were talking about something called "the Internet." Hugh's experience in desktop publishing had made him comfortable with new technologies, and while many pooh-poohed the Internet in its early stages, Hugh and his boss, SXSW managing director Roland Swenson, saw the unseen future, and it was a future in digital bits: the Internet, CD-ROMs, start-ups, e-commerce, games, and virtual experiences.

An innovative team player sees the future and takes swings at it, which is precisely what Hugh and his coworkers did. In 1994, Hugh led the launch of separate film and multimedia programs for SXSW. Music was still the festival's main draw, and he knew they could always end the technology component: "If it doesn't pick up, we can always kill it" was the guiding mantra.

After a slow march forward, SXSW Multimedia, later renamed SXSW Interactive, began gaining real traction. And so did the film component of the festival, with worldwide debuts and movie stars mingling with the rock stars who now mingled with Internet geeks. SXSW Interactive, which Hugh has directed for more than 20 years, soon became the major festival mover, largely owing to Hugh's stewardship. Today it draws more attendees and more buzz than either the music or film portions.

Hugh is an example of how the Inside/Upside Hustle brings a satisfaction that comes in part from the long slog—the test of endurance that requires us to do the little things each day most people won't. What keeps Hugh going at SXSW? "You get stories about people who attend the festival and got a job out of the event, landed an investor, found a cofounder, met a new best friend, or even met their spouse," he says. In other words, Hugh has built a massive and wonderful honeypot.

Today, Hugh Forrest without SXSW is not Hugh Forrest. And SXSW without Hugh Forrest is not SXSW, either. Their identities and growth are intertwined.

Even after roughly a quarter of a century at SXSW, Hugh feels more driven now than ever. "SXSW needs more attention than it did before," he says. "Twenty years ago, the summers were pretty boring. Now [it's] a year-round event. It's about the transition and the move forward to see what happens next. The only thing I care about is that the attendees enjoy their time and have a positive experience." For Hugh, the bulk of his time is spent in planning sessions and panels and setting the environment for people to meet each other, run into each other, and create new opportunities.

SXSW has opened numerous doors and continues to open more—and Hugh is still surprised by its success. That people heap awards, honors, and praise on SXSW is testament to Hugh and his team's dedication to building the community. The friendships and relationships make it worthwhile. Again, these come only through the dedication of the steady hustle.

As for any perceived lack of ambition early on, Hugh's is now clear: He's found his niche and his hidden talents in directing programming and panels for SXSW Interactive, and he has been a steady, disciplined culture maker and a collaborative builder for the past 20-plus years. And he keeps climbing. Hugh's hustle is directed by a desire to create not only a context of opportunity for others to share but a celebration of the future itself. The Inside/Upside Hustle has been about building his future simultaneously.

Secret of Hugh's Success

In case you're wondering about Hugh's secrets to success, he recommends two things in particular that work for him.

1. He answers hundreds of e-mails each day in 2 *minutes or less*. And he has his team adopt this rapid-response customer-service approach.

2. He's a disciplined sleeper who goes to bed at 9 p.m. each night and rises at 4 a.m.

Hugh finds he can do more in the morning, and getting e-mails out the door is one way he clears space for other priorities. This gives him more time to dedicate to meetings and leading his team's focus on making SXSW Interactive not only an amazing creativity- and idea-exchanging event but a top-notch customer-service event where he can foster and grow the community.

Festivals such as SXSW are incredibly challenging and unique culture-making experiences that require a well-run organization. They're naturally magnets for luck. But so too are small, medium, and large companies with smart leaders who care about cultivating talent from within and developing loyal teams bound to careers. These are the places you want to look as you consider your own Inside/Upside Hustle. If you're in one of these organizations already, then the only thing you need to do is communicate with your manager, lay out a growth path, and create a plan for transitioning you into a new and hopefully more challenging role. If you're not in a company that wants to see you grow, then it's probably a good idea to begin looking elsewhere and working on your Inside/Outside Hustle.

3. The Inside/Outside Hustle

In 2010, bestselling author Sunni Brown received a frightening phone call. The caller informed her that she had been invited to speak on the main stage at TED in Long Beach, California.

TED, if you're unfamiliar, is short for Technology, Entertainment, and Design and is among the most exclusive conferences in the world. Its audience is comprised of established and aspiring innovators, along with a who's who of the technorati who happily pay four figures to be edified in captivating short talks by today's leading thinkers, educators, artists, and scientists.

If you're so lucky as to be invited to speak, you'd better deliver the best 10-minute talk of your life, because it's one thing to give a presentation before a corporate audience, and it's entirely another thing to capture the imagination of ex-presidents, billionaires, and Nobel laureates.

Stage fright? Nah. How about stage terror? Stage panic? Stage nausea? After that phone call, it was all of above.

Contemplating the invitation, Sunni realized that her hustle had led her down such a different—and colorful—rabbit hole than that of most of the people she grew up around.

Make no bones about it; Sunni grew up in depressive childhood poverty in an East Texas trailer park. Institutional ignorance, learned helplessness, mental illness, and legacy trauma were all part of her childhood milieu.

While most of her friends sank deeper into hopeless Cycles of Suck, Sunni escaped into books and ideas. As a young girl, she nurtured her mind with the stories she read and emptied her piggy bank paying off the incessant fines racked up from all the overdue books she'd borrowed from the local library.

Looking back, the overdue fees were her first investment in herself, as she worked her way from an impoverished childhood to graduate school at University of Texas at Austin, where she first floated to her professors the value of visual models as a way to help simplify and explain the complexity of policy work.

Once Sunni had wrapped up her master's work, by now disillusioned by the reality of public policy work, she ventured west to the San Francisco Bay Area to seek greener pastures. She found work at a consulting firm that specialized in solving complex problems through design thinking and graphic recording.

Sunni's time on the West Coast was an education that would open up opportunities and pay big, unseen dividends later. It was there where she further developed her innate talents in the language of visual thinking, and it was through dedicated doing that she found her form.

Graphic recording and visual thinking are far more than just drawing snappy pictures. Graphic recording is a method of using a combination of images, words, and shapes to help teams and working groups capture shared visions and solve problems. It helps people "see what they mean." Sunni's experience led to a deeper discovery of her talents, and she *honed* her creative talents in visual thinking for problem-solving in large companies.

Client feedback was off the charts. Clients found Sunni not only delightful, moreover she was exceptionally effective and they made sure to hire her company for ongoing engagements. Finally, Sunni had a sense of fitting into a professional community and excelling in her role—by facilitating breakthroughs for her clients and generating more revenue for her company.

She knew that this was deeply rewarding work designed for her talents—and where she belonged. Sunni had found her professional groove. Emboldened by her success with the company's clients, Sunni made a case for a raise, an Inside/Upside Hustle opportunity.

But walking out of her boss's office that fateful day, a stunned Sunni fought back tears. Her case for a raise had been met with the equivalent of a cold bucket of water to her face.

As much as she loved her job, Sunni knew she couldn't stay at a company that didn't respect her hard work and talents. She packed up, left the Bay Area, and moved back to Texas, where she had the support of friends and family—and another opportunity.

Upon arrival in Austin, Sunni had already secured a well-paid, "low-risk" position working for a state agency that dealt with workplace insurance—she knew it wasn't her calling, but it would tide her by as she licked her wounds and considered next steps.

Sunni started the job on Monday and by 2 p.m. that afternoon; she knew she had jumped out of the frying pan into the fire. On Friday, she submitted her resignation. The job had not turned out to be a temporary waypoint, but two steps backward in her career.

As financially constrained as she was, she couldn't see herself biding her time there for even another week. It was the last time she'd work as an employee of that company—and any other company.

Sunni's strong sense of individuality might have been a clue that the Inside/Outside Hustle could serve her well. If you're a creative or entrepreneurially minded doer feeling stifled by growth ceilings or organizational bureaucracy, or if you're driven by unconventional curiosity, this may be just the pathway you're looking for too.

Sunni knew she was ready to make her own move—*outside the organization*—into the great unknown to forward her career. Scraping together what little money she had—$850—she started hustling. She called on contacts and pitched any and all local graphic recording opportunities. She won a $6,000 contract and continued from there, relentlessly working on her pitching and sharing her impressively growing portfolio. She hustled no fewer than 100 lunch meetings that first year, which led to enough business for financial stability.

Now, firmly on her feet, she pitched the idea of graphically recording the keynotes at SXSW Interactive (hello, Hugh Forrest), which helped put her graphic recordings (sometimes referred to as large-scale *infodoodles*) of panels and presentations on the radar of the cool kids and companies in attendance at the festival.

Her work's strategic exposure led to a significant leveling up of her business. With better and more leads every day, she was no longer just treading water. She commanded higher fees for consulting, speaking, and leading workshops—anywhere in the world. And she did, from an opportunity in Saudi Arabia with Saudi royalty, creating infodoodles alongside Bill Clinton and Tony Blair, to graphically recording a young, shy Mark Zuckerberg.

As her career trajectory steepened, Sunni sought to share her expertise in ways other than in-person graphic recordings, so she authored her first book, *Gamestorming*.

With her hard-won successes, Sunni had betrayed herself to stay true to herself: where she had come from didn't dictate with whom she would work and what sort of impact her work would have.

In Long Beach, a few hours before her scheduled TED talk, still shaking with fear at the prospect of getting on stage—she summoned strength, confidence, and satisfaction knowing that she was no longer that bespectacled 13-year-old girl hiding in the library. And that 13-year-old Sunni would be proud of what Sunni had overcome. And certainly wouldn't let Sunni chicken out of the greatest opportunity of her life.

That day, in front of Bill Gates, Sunni delivered a wonderfully quirky talk that has drawn views from more than a million people around the world. A wonderfully quirky woman giving a wonderfully quirky talk can *only* bring about Quirky Luck. Her TED success brought her acclaim and the attention of a major New York publisher. She went on to publish her second book, based on her TED talk, called *The Doodle Revolution*. Moreover, conquering her fears and delivering a TED talk had been one of her 10-year goals.

She had accomplished it in only 2 years.

Today, she continues to lead her consultancy, write books, and rewrite the rules of her work and life.

Sunni is living proof that hustling brings money, meaning, and momentum. She's not an unhappy employee or a starving artist. She's a self-directed entrepreneur constantly working in the pursuit of her craft, creativity, and curiosity and looking for new horizons to explore, educate, and push the world forward in her own distinct way.

The Inside/Outside Hustle requires that you leave the comforts of someone else's company, allow your entrepreneurial gear to kick in, and absorb the terror as risk taking hits you like a ton of bricks. It's where you do your own thing to launch in a meaningful way, which might mean beginning with a small consulting gig or side hustle, or a new entrepreneurial venture entirely, like a start-up.

The downside is that this pathway comes *without any guarantees,* and it places a greater responsibility on you to develop the business, operate it, and sustain it. The upside is that you have more control over your destiny; from making a schedule to setting rates, you decide for yourself. There's no paycheck and no boss, and generally there are few rules. Autonomy is a staple perk, and major hustle, movement, and follow-through will be required every day, as you're now the owner of a new enterprise. You are the captain of your ship and master of your fate in a pronounced way.

Whether in a small business, start-up, consultancy, solopreneurship, or in your own studio as a working artist, you'll quickly need to find your place in a sea of competition. That means constantly upping your game and adding to your Personal Opportunity Portfolio (POP, which we'll cover in Chapter 9) through newly acquired skills. It also means learning to leap without a clear landing.

To pull off a successful Inside/Outside Hustle, you'll need courage, a firm belief that you can and will succeed, and confidence that you're on the right track. *Even if it means ultimately failing.* The real reason you make this kind of aggressive move is to be honest with yourself that you've likely hit a growth ceiling—*you'll know it when you hit one*—and you are ready to take your talents elsewhere. Or you want to start surfacing latent talents not under development in your current situation.

When you hit the growth ceiling, you will see the writing on the wall: There's no space for your advancement in the company and no room to wiggle into a new role—even if it's a sideways move. Maybe the competition is too tough or you lack the credentials or internal confidence to get to the next level? Maybe a change of industry would benefit you? If you're not a yes-person or you have personality-clash issues, if you can't find a manager who supports you or you are simply a poor fit for the company's growth strategy, then it's time to go. There's nothing left for you to say, do, or accomplish, and even if there was, the risk of staying put far exceeds the rewards of moving on.

So what do you do? You move from company A (inside) to company B (outside) or you start your own company (an outside play all the way). This is the path of the person who opts out of their old role to take on a new one with bigger responsibilities, like becoming an entrepreneur or small business owner. Whatever the case, it means moving from the old, known (inside) situation to the new, unknown (outside) one. At first, it might feel terrifying, and it will involve a small dose (or many small doses) of pain to be sure, but it always ends up being a liberating experience

If you think the Inside/Outside Hustle may be the pathway forward for you, think of people you know, friends who've left comfortable jobs to redefine themselves on their own terms in an outside hustle. Talk to them. Whether they've started a food truck or their own side business on Etsy, find out if they have any regrets about the experience. What did they learn about themselves in the process? Are they better or worse financially, emotionally, and energetically? You might be surprised.

4. The Outside/Upside Hustle

We reserve the final hustle pathway for the boldest, most dedicated, and luckiest hustlers among us. The route they follow is beset by oblique ascents that require a bigger energetic push than the other three pathways combined—and an appetite for even bigger doses of risk.

To succeed here, one needs a firm commitment to action and manufacturing all four varieties of luck. And sometimes this way forward means working on the fringes of the rules, making them up, or even breaking them as you go, so that you can beat the odds and change the world in a positive way.

Freely enterprising, entrepreneurial, and high-achieving artists flourish on this course. And as observers, it's our favorite and arguably the most adventurous, exciting, and serendipitous of the four pathways. It's the Outside/Upside Hustle. This is the way celebrated entrepreneurs like Bill Gates, Oprah Winfrey, and others have seen the unseen opportunities and made their way to find more momentum, money, and meaning than most could ever dream of encountering. It's a pathway that's heroic, crazy, and even epic—one that, if traversed successfully, always leads to discovery, reinvention, and massive breakthroughs along the way.

Some people are just cut out for the rigors of the Outside/Upside Hustle: Think about famous bands who've reshaped music and made a fortune, like the Rolling Stones. Or consider any one of the hosts of the show *Shark Tank*. Each host started with little or nothing and turned it into something remarkable. People on this path take lots of swings and make their own luck by exploiting the gaps in the market and leveraging advantages. They perform at high levels, and they build imaginative products, services, and experiences that dominate the market. They fundamentally see the world differently, and they wish to make a big impact. Their motivations, like yours and ours, are to build a constant stream of money, meaning, and momentum on their own terms, and to play by their own rules as much as possible.

To illustrate the path, let's look at John Paul DeJoria, a man who has dedicated his life to the pursuit of the Outside/Upside Hustle. In case you do not recognize the name, he's a celebrated bearded billionaire businessman, an optimist, and philanthropist with an unmistakable charm, warm glow, and Hollywood smile.

He's been able to succeed on this exalted pathway multiple times, driven not just by an iron will but by doubling down on his innate talents and by a burning desire to give back and make a difference in the world.

DeJoria got his first taste of entrepreneurship growing up in East Los Angeles. As a child, he sold Christmas cards and newspapers to help support his family. He also got a taste of tragedy: His parents divorced when he was just 2 years old. He and his brother were in foster care during the week and only saw their working mother on the weekends.

After high school, he bounced around from the Navy to a series of unfulfilling temporary jobs leaving him temporarily homeless but, as we'll see, not hopeless.

Even though he hadn't run out of *un*luck, DeJoria sensed that his talents, without question, were rooted in his abilities of charm, persuasion, and sales. Not just any sort of sales—but sales of high-quality, differentiated products that he personally shaped.

Seeing a growth opportunity, he found his way into the hair product and hair care space as a district sales manager for Redken. All was well until he was fired over a disagreement. And John Paul, once again, was out of a job.

During his time at Redken, he and hairstylist Paul Mitchell had developed a friendship.

And, well, what better time than after being fired to start a new company?

As he recounted in an interview, "Paul never did business. I never did hair. So we were perfect partners."

John Paul Mitchell Systems was born.

With a mere $700 investment, a convertible car, and a rolodex of contacts, the two men launched a new and better hair care line, beginning with only three products.

DeJoria personally drove sales, going from salon to salon to sell the new product line and charming customers to secure the future of his fledgling company.

While the company began to gain traction with its high-end hair care products, his family life began to crumble. He found himself homeless again, this time with his young son.

They slept in his car and scraped by while continuing to hustle John Paul Mitchell Systems products. Their initial financial goal was to simply be able to pay their bills on time. Once they did that and established a small profit of $2,000, DeJoria knew that he was onto something big.

As everyone who ever watched TV in the 1980s knows, the ever-charismatic, pony-tailed DeJoria became the public face of the company, and the company blossomed into a highly lucrative empire valued at $900 million.

Perhaps that was a fluke? A 1 in 900 million swing? Nah, DeJoria knew exactly what he was meant to do and was ready to take another product to the next level with his idiosyncratic style of personal marketing.

A longtime fan of tequila, DeJoria bemoaned that most tequila suffered from low quality ingredients and poor distillation methods. Just like the hair care market had been primed for premium products, the tequila market was ready for a better product that tequila enthusiasts could savor, not just shoot down.

In 1989, DeJoria and partners launched Patrón Spirits International. But just in case you haven't stepped foot in a bar in the last 25 years, Patrón Tequila is one of the most successful and iconic brands in the spirits world. Much like John Paul DeJoria himself.

These days, he's a self-made billionaire who continues to run multiple companies, while also producing films and running numerous philanthropic nonprofits that tackle educational, environmental, and social concerns.

DeJoria's motto is "Success unshared is failure." It's a message that brings authentic money, meaning, and momentum to his life's work—and impacts many lives in the process.

DeJoria's story and successes involve many factors—dogged persistence, seeing unseen opportunities in hair care and spirits markets, but most striking to us is DeJoria's discovery of and belief in his own talents to own his dreams and make his future POP.

The Outside/Upside Hustle is clearly *not* for everyone. As Tesla Motors founder Elon Musk says, "You need to have a high pain threshold" for it to work out. It's a journey of astonishing adversity and, if it works out successfully, amazing advantages. More often than not, it's a rocky road on which most entrepreneurs and artists fail. Even those with the grandest of vision can get devoured on this pathway due to poor execution, bad luck, and other factors. So persistence is key. Those who emerge successfully get to redefine the old and invent the new; build great empires in the rubble of smaller, outdated, or inefficient ones; and create a culture- and a game-changing legacy that touches peoples' lives and changes the world.

No matter what type of hustle works best for your situation, and there may be more than one of these four from which to choose, if you want to draw on one of the most effective ways to strengthen yourself and improve your opportunities, you must put yourself on a pathway that leads to adventure and the excitement it brings. Over a lifetime, the benefits of growth are immeasurable and will help you build and grow your own dream as you move through one, or many, of the hustles on the Fourfold Path. The more experience and the more new challenges you undertake, the bigger will be the rewards—and the closer you will get to owning your dream, the destiny of "what could be."

Before you start mapping your strategy for making your next move, it's worth asking the question: Might there be a tactical way to build your portfolio *and* help hasten your prospects for a successful upside adventure? Might there be a way to stack the deck in favor of your future?

PART THREE
HABITS

"Things start out as hopes and end up as habits."
—LILLIAN HELLMAN

9

MAKE YOUR FUTURE POP

"Enthusiasm is the electricity of life. How do you get it? You act enthusiastic until you make it a habit."

—Gordon Parks

POP Like a Personal IPO

Often when we hear excited rumblings in the media about a company gearing up for a major initial public offering (IPO) on Wall Street, we think of an innovative global software player with amazing technology, like Google and its powerful search engine, which we use every day. Or we think of an Internet service company that's extremely well positioned in its category, with many millions of users, brilliant algorithms, and an unbeatable pricing strategy, such as Amazon and its warehouses of easily deliverable goods—even on Sunday. Or maybe it's a massively popular consumer product company, like Apple with its stellar design for computers, iPhones, and iEverything else. We look for something extremely useful, something that changes the game, something exciting that will impact our experience in the world. And sometimes it's a company that offers a mix of these qualities.

Typically, we don't think of a food company, let alone a macaroni and cheese maker, as a bona fide player in the big-money, high-flying IPO space. But it's time we rethink that assumption.

In March 2012, shares for Annie's Homegrown went out in an IPO on the New York Stock Exchange. Up to that point, the little, Berkeley, California–based foods company had performed well, and was mainly known for two things: its tasty organic macaroni and cheese sold in supermarkets and retail stores and its commitment to a socially responsible mission of nourishing families with the simple, healthy foods they love.

But on that day in March, Annie's would become known for another reason.

On the day of the IPO, Annie's saw its shares officially priced and sold at around $19 per share. The next morning, things changed dramatically and for the better. As the trading day began, shares spiked, trading at more than $31 per share. Investors flocked to the stock, driving the price higher still. By close of the stock market, the per-share stock price had nearly doubled, settling in at just shy of $36.

The 89 percent leap from the $19 IPO price the day before was astounding. Amazingly, Annie's enjoyed the finest performance of any IPO since the initial offering of the renowned business-oriented social networking company LinkedIn in 2011.

With its stock popping, Annie's market value approached $600 million.

This infusion of value helped Annie's pay its early investors handsomely and raise significant money for expanding operations. A few hundred million in cash never hurts, and now Annie's Homegrown could compete with the big boys, the multinational consumer-food players. The company began to diversify its already top-rate offerings and place bets on its future by expanding its product line and doubling down on the winning formula it had already created. Annie's was no longer playing small-time.

In fact, the company's stock continued to soar, returning more than 100 percent since the IPO, riding on the quality of its products and the consumer demand for healthy, organic, and natural foods. Less than 3 years later, General Mills, the juggernaut foods maker, acquired Annie's for $820 million.

It's absolutely clear that an IPO was the right move for Annie's. Financial investors in the public markets could now find a great growth company in which to place their money. Had Annie's stayed private, the growth story would have been harder to forecast—to be sure, there are investors that specialize in investing in private companies, but it's a lot smaller world with a lot less money sloshing around.

Annie's stock popped because they did the preparation work for the IPO—they delivered the goods, did their homework, and paced themselves so that they went public at a moment when the market and their infrastructure were poised for them to succeed. How can you follow in Annie's footsteps and rapidly increase your value and growth opportunities in the world? You need to have a clear plan for how to bake-in, create, and take advantage of your best personal opportunities. Lucky for you, we have a plan right here: It's called POP, or the Personal Opportunity Portfolio. This is what will help people and companies find you and invest in your success.

Opportunity Architecture: Hustle's Substructure

It's time we nudge you a bit further down the path to glory, from *thinking* about moving forward to undertaking a sustained process of *actually* moving forward. This means transitioning from blue-sky *dreaming* to hands and feet on the ground *doing*. To make this shift a reality, you'll be putting into practice the Three Unseen Laws of Hustle from Chapter 6.

1. **Hustle in Your Heart:** Do Something That *Moves* You. This imbues you with energy, enthusiasm, and excitement. Don't worry about so-called passion, just set the wheels of possibility in motion.

2. **Hustle in Your Head:** Keep Your Head Up and Your Eyes Open. Embrace risk and look for hidden opportunity and ways to manufacture luck. A little luck goes a long way.

3. **Hustle in Your Habits:** Seal the Deal and Make It
   Real. Turn an opportunity into a valuable exchange.
   Concrete transactions generate growth and upside
   optionality, and proof.

Those are the principles, and POP, your Personal Opportunity Portfolio, makes up the practices, ensuring that you have all of the elements you need to move forward. Your POP exists to capture and broadcast the sum total of your life's work: your professional credibility, the relationships you've formed and contacts you've made in the world, as well as the projects and jobs you take on and the potential you grow into over time. You develop your POP throughout your life as you hustle to generate more money, meaning, and momentum. Ultimately, POP becomes a mirror reflection of you. It helps you define your contributions and authentic identity in the world.

Think of POP as the single best investment you can ever make. Why? Because it is an investment in Y-O-U. And if we reflect back to the notion of owning your dream, POP becomes the bridge that unites your dreaming with your doing.

The experience of building POP serves as a device for hormetic resilience, giving you small doses of pain for bigger gains as you practice hustle. Inevitably, as you get knocked down, you'll stay strong and hustle on because you've diversified. If you recall from Chapter 3, the more we diversify our risk—making several smart bets rather than just one— the more success and luck we enable. Less risk is more risky, and POP is about placing more targeted risks, professionally and creatively, in your basket—strike that, in your *baskets*—for the long haul. It doesn't mean you won't fail occasionally; it just gives you more at-bats to find your way to success. And when you fail, it makes recovery a piece of cake.

Like us, you've probably been asked countless times, "What do you do?" and felt unsure or even doubtful of your answer. Well, POP helps us answer that, too. From an identity-framing standpoint, when we execute POP successfully, it says much about our past, present, and future, where we've been and where we're going in life—and what matters to us. POP satisfies our needs for validation, attracts people to us, gives us deep access to peers and experts, and directs us toward mentors as well.

The POP we build helps fulfill our desire for growth and enhances our luck as we confidently take more action. It pushes us from *what we could be* to *what we will become* in terms of our professional and even personal identities. To develop POP is to give yourself permission to hustle. And that's what you must do if you are to own your dreams, choose your adventures, and grow into the person you're destined to become.

The One Habit That Rules Them All: The 10-Minute Rule

Developing your POP might strike you as an overwhelming prospect, like taming a wild animal. We want you to know it's not: There's a simple way to work on it and in the process develop a powerful habit for your hustle. The best part is it takes a mere 10 minutes per day.

If life has taught the three of us anything, it is this: Getting started is the single most difficult aspect of doing anything worthwhile. Not finding a good idea. Not executing.

Think about your life. From mundane tasks like washing dishes after dinner to going for a run to getting up without hitting snooze at 5 a.m. fourteen times to writing a book about hustle, it is the thought that is vastly more painful than the actual task. Always has been, and always will be.

How many times have you groaned at the thought of going to the gym only to find that once you are all of 7 minutes into your workout, you not only feel absolutely fantabulous, you question why you even hesitated in the first place?

How absurd! And inescapable *and* human. As irrational creatures of habit, many of us tend to put off small breaks in our routine to do the things that we need most. Like getting to bed early when we know we need rest; opting for a healthy meal when we've felt bloated for

14 days in a row; not prioritizing quiet time for reading; forgetting to unplug from our Internet devices for even a day; putting off a work task or home chore that's nipping at our conscious—whatever it may be.

To alleviate the inevitable feelings of self-imposed friction, what we call the anti-hustle, we have a simple solution—maybe even brilliant in its simplicity.

The 10-Minute Rule states that instead of contemplating and delaying, simply do something that moves you—sans judgment—for 10 minutes and then evaluate.

Do for 10 minutes, *then* evaluate. (Not evaluate for 10 minutes and never do.)

Say you want to exercise but also want to talk yourself out of exercising right now. Stop talking, stop deliberating, and instead start walking briskly or, better, go to the gym and pick any exercise machine. Just do it. Ten minutes is all we're asking for. Go, get started!

Maybe you have a presentation to craft for a meeting tomorrow afternoon but would rather play Ping-Pong or a game on your phone or check Facebook or Twitter to search for hilarious animated GIFs. Instead, plant yourself and focus on one thing: Jot down the key message of the presentation, work out the points you'll need to cover. Do it in 10 minutes or less. Set the countdown clock on your phone or watch if need be.

It's a simple way of staying productive, present, and focused in the moment, and in a place of near constant momentum. Putting the 10-Minute Rule into practice saves us time and headaches and allows us to quickly make decisions about how to prioritize and allocate our resources and energy by circumventing our propensity to overthink.

Benefits of the 10-Minute Rule

While we find numerous advantages to employing the 10-Minute Rule, there are three main benefits.

1. **Rapid Productivity: Have something critical and essential—or even annoying—to do? Tackle it immediately, as in right now.** Ten minutes is all you

have to get moving. Make a quick list of a few items, plot them on your calendar or to-do list, and pick any one of them to start.

Have a phone call to make? Smile and dial. An e-mail to send? Craft it and get it out quickly, like Hugh Forrest. A proposal that needs to get out the door and to your clients? Wrap it up. A pitch to practice to win new business? Talk through it in front of a mirror for 10 minutes. Or maybe it's just scheduling a brief meeting to close a deal. Cement it on your and your client's calendars now. You have something that must get done today—we all do—and now is better than later. So just do it, get moving, get 'er done—and done now. Start the day with a burst of the 10-Minute Rule. Track your progress for a week to see how this helps you.

2. **Unfettered Presence:** Ever felt distracted or even powerless against the forces of overwhelm and overload? Do you find yourself torn between tracking your American Express expenses, taking a peek at TMZ, and responding to more text messages and social media invites than you can count?

   Use the 10-Minute Rule to get undistracted and be present with one task at a time. Own it. That means sitting or standing upright with good posture, practicing steady nasal breathing, and staying present with the task at hand. If you're working on your smartphone, use only one app. If you're on another device, the same rule applies—do only one thing at a time. Breathe it in, focus on it, and finish it—and only it. Then move on. Give yourself 10 minutes to exert real control over your destiny.

3. **Friction-Free Persistence:** It's been said that "God is action." Think of your 10-minute session as a spiritual practice. It's the Zen-like daily practice of mindful

doing. It's a meditation, a short burst of effective, non-judgmental output. You are a monk in your temple of doing, whether it's a monastery or a cubicle. You're committed to pursuing opportunity and enjoying small doses of gain every day.

The short time required forces you into a focused and disciplined bubble, after which you can decide if you want to pursue the question, problem, or pursuit of opportunity for a longer period. We know someone who created a sign for his office that read, DO NOT DISTURB. I'M IN THE TEMPLE OF DOING. You might follow suit.

The Four Pieces of POP

In our research for this book, we looked at success models far and wide—in our own work and in the work of peers, proven entrepreneurs, seasoned professionals, and thriving organizations. We consulted with experts and pored over scores of books, online studies, and scientific data points. We had anecdotal discussions with fellow thought leaders and folks who actively push the world forward. And we reflected on our own journeys, too, asking questions of each other that we had difficulty answering at first.

After trial and error, we arrived at a scaled-down, simplified model for our truth about how we successfully navigate the real world and build our money, meaning, and momentum. It became readily apparent that a career is composed of four key elements, like pieces of pie, that either bolster or break your future, sustain or stifle your growth, and contribute to the lives of others in exponential ways. Your Personal Opportunity Portfolio is built on Potential, People, Projects, and Proof. It's these four buckets that you fill as you hustle. You can add to these in any order or sequence you choose, and in any amount. The beauty is, wherever you are in your life, it's likely you've already been filling your pieces of pie.

Let's take a deeper look at each of these four critical pieces.

POP: Your Personal Opportunity Portfolio

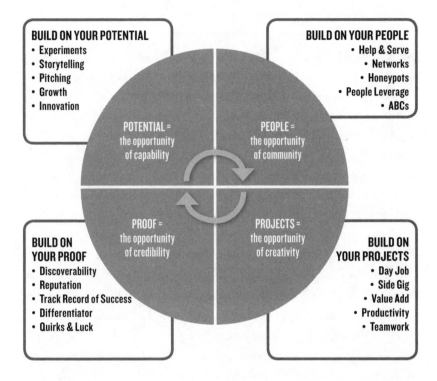

BUILD ON YOUR POTENTIAL
- Experiments
- Storytelling
- Pitching
- Growth
- Innovation

POTENTIAL =
the opportunity
of capability

BUILD ON YOUR PEOPLE
- Help & Serve
- Networks
- Honeypots
- People Leverage
- ABCs

PEOPLE =
the opportunity
of community

PROOF =
the opportunity
of credibility

**BUILD ON
YOUR PROOF**
- Discoverability
- Reputation
- Track Record of Success
- Differentiator
- Quirks & Luck

PROJECTS =
the opportunity
of creativity

**BUILD ON
YOUR PROJECTS**
- Day Job
- Side Gig
- Value Add
- Productivity
- Teamwork

1. The Potential Piece: In most cases, you aren't hired for a job simply based on your professional identity and the boundaries of your résumé. Those things matter, but more important to employers are the unseen qualities, the values and possibilities yet to come. Employers intuit when there's "room for growth in there," space for your energetic contribution to their company or cause. Getting chosen for a job or a project is about aligning your potential with a company's or client's needs and solving problems they can't solve. *Your future is about capability,* and this piece addresses your need to discover new talents and identify the strengths, growth, autonomy, self-direction, and purpose you need to get to the next step of your journey.

To provide an example: Neil might focus on growing his skills in a new product area each month. He'll run an experiment and measure what works and doesn't through his audience's responsiveness and his ability to drive online traffic to, say, a blog post about a nutritional supplement or a new tech gadget on the market, or to test a new marketing concept for a car company.

Patrick actively engages through stories. At 9:30 a.m., he's actively pitching a deal for his start-up company in the audio technology space. By noon, he's working through a slide deck or talking through opportunities to consult with corporate clients. In the afternoon, he's polishing up a talk he'll be giving.

Understanding your potential helps you solve the problem of moving from *what you are* to *what you can become*. It guides you, ultimately, to what you do that will lead you to your why, your deeper purpose. It's the statement that confidently says, "I'm a work in progress," and it lays out your unique skills, talents, hidden luck, attitude, and resources.

2. The People Piece: What is the strongest source of opportunity and luck in your life and work? Why, it's you and other people, of course! And that's precisely what this piece of POP addresses: *the relationships you develop in your real-world and global online community and the opportunity these can yield for you and others*. The People Piece speaks to those you know and those you'll need to know. This piece represents the sum total of your social capital, your reach and depth in your personal and professional networks.

More important, the People Piece specifically deals with how you navigate or operate within your community to *help* and contribute to the needs, wants, lives, and work of others, by serving them and *connecting them to other people*. You become a bridge linking people and opportunity. People are the "net" result of the "work" you do to build community.

Neil works on his People Piece every day. Wherever he might be for the week, he is constantly practicing literal elevator pitching to neighbors or guests. Patrick has an uncanny ability to see connections between people and projects and actively introduces people whenever he gets an opportunity. For example, he introduced Neil and Jonas.

3. The Projects Piece: What you *presently do* and how you do it says something hugely personal about you—suggesting both your interests *and* your ability to execute work at a high level, as well as the choices that make you unique, interesting, and even remarkable. The projects you are involved in are *a statement of action*. It's important that you tackle every project in a way that shows your own greatest skills and abilities, whether you're the founder or an entry-level assistant. *Every* job has a benefit, and the Projects Piece indicates how you should look for tasks that suit the skills you're trying to hone and also tackle jobs in a manner that fully demonstrates who you are as a capable, creative doer.

Projects are how you sustain your hustle, building money, meaning, and momentum. Through projects you speak to doing what moves you, while bringing in money to sustain your momentum through activity, output, and results.

Neil focuses on any number of projects throughout each day, from running an existing start-up to pitching a new company, driving online traffic, adding a new blog post, or responding to a hundred e-mails. Jonas might look at five new projects a month that vary in complexity and choose one that maps most tightly to his skill set, interests, and talents—and aligns with his values. Projects are about everything from how you express your creativity to what your day job or career looks like to which experiments you're running to what side work you're doing and so forth.

4. The Proof Piece: More than anything, the Proof Piece is *a definitive statement of your credibility,* and it speaks to your reputation. It points people to where they can actually bear witness to the fruits of your labor. Proof solves two major types of problems: professional and personal. Professionally, it sets you apart from the herd and clarifies your ability to deliver. In a world where people are mostly talkers, Proof is all about the show—it's your show and your way of telling. Personally, Proof enables you to unequivocally say to the world, "I built X," "I did Y," "I made Z." It *raises* your perceived value in the world. When done well, it gives you a platform for influencing others, a way for you to wow them.

Neil's blog, Quick Sprout, is a shining example. Attracting millions of readers every month and providing valued content and eliciting active feedback, it shows proof of Neil's work and success to date. Patrick's previous book, *The Lean Entrepreneur*, has been translated into multiple languages and is beloved by thousands of readers worldwide, leading to a spot on the *New York Times* bestseller list.

The act of creating anything is, in effect, a rebellion against the universe. The universe tends toward entropy, toward more randomness and more disorder. When you manufacture proof by creating something new, you reduce entropy and increase order. That signal is one that all humans are tuned to receive. It is exactly why we marvel at ancient structures such as the Pantheon in Rome. This temple, built under the direction of the Roman emperor Hadrian in AD 126, features an impressive, unreinforced concrete dome—still the largest of its kind nearly 2,000 years after its construction!

Proof is alchemy; it's how 2 + 2 = 5. The Pantheon is literally just tons and tons of ancient Roman concrete, yet walking inside you experience an unavoidable awe. The physicality of the Pantheon stands as irrefutable proof of its creators' ability to make and to create in the face of an uncaring universe. We're not suggesting you need to create another Pantheon—just that tangible proof allows others to experience your abilities of creation directly, and that is the most powerful signal of all, one that draws allies, friends, colleagues, luck, and opportunities your way.

Entrepreneur Elon Musk recently tweeted the following.

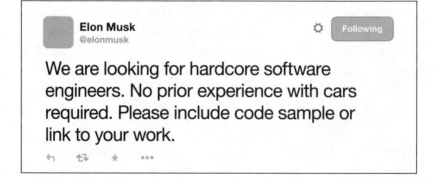

Elon Musk
@elonmusk
Following

We are looking for hardcore software engineers. No prior experience with cars required. Please include code sample or link to your work.

Elon wasn't asking for résumés, he was asking for Proof.

Proof is also a way for you to dispel any self-doubt that you carry and suspend skepticism or resistance you receive from others. When you display your work through Proof, you escape the antiquated rat race of unread résumés. Proof is your opportunity magnet: It attracts people to you by saying, unequivocally, "I've arrived."

In sum, the four pieces of POP give you capability in the form of Potential, community in the form of People, creativity in the form of Projects, and credibility in the form of Proof. They require focus, urgency, ambition, and, above all, optimism and enthusiasm. Those are what will sustain your momentum for the rest of your life. Keep in mind, you're likely to live at least 77.98 years. Maybe even 81.24 years. That gives you miles to go.

Now, you might be thinking, as we were when we set out on a mission to discover POP, Well, isn't this all patently obvious?

Of course it is!

Yes, I need to grow my Proof Piece and deepen my credibility.

Come on, I can't do anything without access to great people whom I can help, and who, in turn, can help connect me to opportunities.

Projects are the lifeblood of opportunity for someone like me— darn right I want to express my creativity and fuel my everyday with work that doesn't just keep me busy but instead fills my life with stimulation, challenge, and learning *and* generates income for me.

And sure, I get the idea that I need to grow—without growth I might not seek new opportunities or look for areas where I can discover my untapped or untested strengths. How will I know what I'm truly great at without exploring my potential?

Sometimes the obvious is hiding in plain sight. POP is a way of helping your hustle take visual shape, of seeing and gauging what you're doing over time and being aware of possible strategic moves that could help you achieve your goals. The beauty of POP is that it's habit forming; it is the essential building block for your dream ownership. It is the self-investment component that we're well aware of beneath the surface of our own lives. Earlier we wrote about surfacing hidden luck and seeing the unseen—finding opportunities where no one else has looked. As you build a POP, you will discover more opportunity than you've ever considered for making money, meaning, and momentum.

The great irony is that POP is like the investment portfolio we mistakenly seek elsewhere. We direct our energy at a rented dream, a life that is less significant than it can be, a time-sucking task we repeat that's meaningless or wasteful. Or we throw money at a stock in a market we can't control. We stand to lose big in both cases if we're not very careful. So why not be more proactive in our pursuits of meaningful investment and make it about ourselves and owning our dreams instead?

We challenge you to start thinking strategically about what your POP might look like and how you can begin engineering your way to the life you want. A POP is yours to build, yours to give to the world, and yours to take from. It's the source of infinite potential. It's time to dig in.

In the next few chapters, we will walk you through the individual pieces in greater detail and share tips for you to build a better, more effective, and more implementable POP. As you seek to achieve your goals, POP will be the focal point for all you do.

Exercise: Simple POP Chart Analysis

As you think about your life and your life's work, visualize your POP as a pie split into four pieces, each one containing one of the key elements of POP. This is your "POP Chart."

What is one significant example you can apply to each of the four pieces? If you don't know yet, simply add a placeholder idea for now. The following questions will help you generate ideas for filling the pieces of your POP Chart.

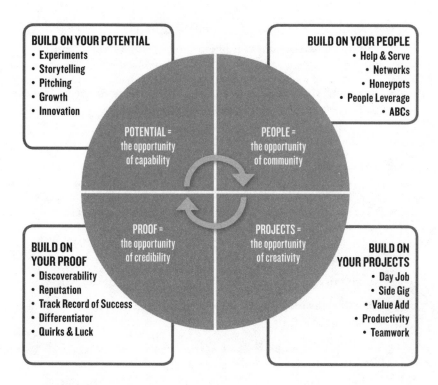

POTENTIAL PIECE

- What skills or talents would you like to grow?

- What experiments are you interested in pursuing?

- What are you doing to explore these interests?

- Are you learning more about your strengths?

- Reflect on the past 2 years of your life. What strengths have been revealed to you, and which strengths are you most interested in and committed to developing profession-ally and personally?

PEOPLE PIECE

- Who are a few significant people in your network whom you have connected to opportunity? What happened?

- Who has connected you to opportunity?

- In your personal and professional life, what networks are you in? Where would you like to be? Are there any organizations that you'd like to be a part of?

- Are there specific people you are looking to connect with who can help you surface more opportunity or see opportunity in new ways?

PROJECTS PIECE

- What is an activity that generates an income for you?

- What is creative about your project?

- What side projects—not including your main income source or job—are you proactively doing?

- What current projects allow you to nurture your curiosity?

- Can you develop a side project or a honeypot that draws people to you?

PROOF PIECE

- What are your current defining proofs? (If the answer is your résumé, keep reading.)

- How do others directly interact with your ability to create?

- What significant work or project have you contributed to?

- Where does it live—how can we find it?

- What impact did it have on you, your team, or your company?

- How does this proof indicate a win or a success?

- What sets you apart from the herd personally and professionally? What makes you most unique, different, and special?

- If you don't have any proofs, what moves you and what are you doing about it?

Want your own POP chart? Download it at HustleGeneration.com.

10

POTENTIAL MAKES YOU POWERFUL

"It's not because things are difficult that we dare not venture. It's because we dare not venture that they are difficult."

—Lucius Annaeus Seneca

At any self-respecting restaurant, there's usually one signature dish that stands out. It makes the chef, her investors and business partners, and the media giggly, gaga, and giddy.

It could be a burger made of 100 percent dry-aged chuck, topped with arugula, caramelized onions, and blue cheese—the best burger ever to come in contact with your lips, at Father's Office in Los Angeles. Perhaps it's a saucy testament to southern cooking, the chicken-fried steak smothered with thick white bacon gravy at Hill's Cafe in Austin, Texas?

These two signature dishes represent the chefs' best intent. They keep the patrons coming back for more. It's what these restaurants hang their hats on. This is a lot like the idea of "potential."

Yet, on either menu, there's more than just the Office Burger or the legendary chicken-fried steak. You have another 20 or more dishes you can order on any given day.

Granted, the restaurateurs hope their respective clients will find their way to the signature dish. But if they don't, if they opt for another choice, the restaurants are happy to accommodate them. Now, any waiter who tells you that everything at their restaurant is outstanding is lying. An honest waiter will distinguish the superstars from the benchwarmers. For the record, the food at both Father's Office and Hill's Cafe is phenomenal, but having a good menu means incorporating a few stellar dishes and adding a few other good and average dishes to provide choice and diversity.

So too, surprisingly, it is with potential. You are able to do a lot of things—some of them well, some of them passably, some of them not so well but you'll give them a try anyway. But you also have your go-to superpower, your talent and strength. That is your signature dish.

It could be your hardball instinct for negotiating deals or your knack for writing dystopian sci-fi novels for Kindle readers. Maybe you are a whiz at understanding the psychology of digital marketing or leasing commercial office space in downtown Chicago. You need to be sure to keep building on your superpower. But you also need to shore up that strength with complementary skills that are not your current strengths nor your weaknesses. Your POP is intended to be built to last over the long haul. Therefore, you must design your potential beyond one strength to avoid too much idiosyncratic risk.

If you're a creative director who is skilled at art direction, where else could you expand your skills? Perhaps sound design? Perhaps copywriting? Add those and now your skill set is more diverse, separating you from the herd. Maybe you're an engineer who is skilled at 3-D modeling—perhaps learning the basics of sales? Not to mention, the useful but boring art of contract review?

The weirdest part of shoring up your strengths with other skills is that you don't even have to be good at these new skills. They're like the coleslaw that comes with the brisket at Patrick's favorite BBQ spot. The brisket is phenomenal, but the coleslaw is just average. Because no one comes for the coleslaw. But a meal of warm brisket and cool coleslaw together is sublime.

Finding things that you can add to your potential is the closest thing to a free lunch you'll ever find.

You just have to do them.

The Secret Equation: Mediocre + Mediocre = Amazing

Scott Adams, the creator of the *Dilbert* comic strip, considers his varied skill set key to his career success. "The secret to my success with *Dilbert* involves my unique *combination* of skills," wrote Adams. "Can you name one other person who has average skills in writing, humor, art, and business? It's a rare mixture. Individually, none of my skills are anywhere near world-class. But combined, they create a powerful market force."

It wasn't any one particular phenomenal skill that made Adams stand out. Rather, it was the combination of a few skills—in all of which he was astoundingly mediocre(!)—that made him uniquely positioned to find success. Adams's success is summed up with what used to pass as an insult: He is the quintessential "jack of all trades and master of none."

Adams claims that he has no, zero, zilch, nada world-class talent—and he's still been incredibly successful. This is why we're so hysterical about the Madness of Mastery and the Perils of Perfection. If you're a Luke Skywalker and exhibit world-class talent along some dimension, by all means, turn that world-class talent into the one and only instrument that helps you generate more money, meaning, and momentum. But if, like most of us, you're more of a Rocky Balboa, that doesn't mean you're doomed to taking second place. In fact, according to Scott Adams, every additional skill you add doubles your odds for success.*

A varied skill set is like a braided rope. The rope is strong even though it may be made up of multiple, sometimes even weak strands. It is the combination of skills, rather than any single skill, that makes you unique and strong.

---

* There's no way of proving this scientifically, but it's a nice rule of thumb to motivate you.

A combination of skills smooths out your risk profile and makes you more resilient to changes in the labor market. It is the combination of skills, again even ones that you are entirely mediocre at, that enables you to take more swings.

More swings, more luck, more hits. More money, more meaning, more momentum.

Grizzly Bears

Two men are hiking through the forest when a ferocious grizzly bear suddenly appears from behind a tree. One of the men quickly drops his backpack, pulls off his hiking boots, and slips on his running shoes.

The other man scoffs, "Don't you know anything? It's impossible to outrun a grizzly bear."

The first man responds, "I don't need to outrun the grizzly bear; I just need to outrun you."

It's an old joke, maybe even ancient. But it illustrates an important aspect of skill acquisition. Adding skills to your Potential Piece isn't about being the best—although that's great, too—it's about being *smart enough to be good enough*.

Potential is about one thing and one thing only: power. Your power. In fact, the word *potential* itself comes to the English language from the Latin word *potentia*, meaning power.

The greater your potential, the greater your power.

How do we develop our potential? There are four steps.

1. We recognize that neither others nor we ourselves are particularly good at recognizing our innate talents.

2. We do lots of different projects in dynamic and varied environments to force our natural talents to the surface.

3. We see through unseen job descriptions; we analyze and track our progress.

4. We surface our talents; we invest in our intrinsic strengths and proceed to ignore our weaknesses.

Most people have never even had a chance for any sort of self-exploration or self-actualization, let alone a deliberate method for achievement. If you follow these four steps, you are already ahead of 90 percent of all of the humans that have ever existed.

At this point, by knowing your strengths and talents and knowing where to invest resources, you are ahead of 98 percent of all of humanity.

To get to 99 percent—where only 1 percent of all of humanity is more fulfilled than you—is frighteningly easy when you remember that you aren't racing against a grizzly bear (perfection) but against other humans. Mediocre humans.

Showing Up

There are whole classes of skills that any hustler can add to their Potential Piece that don't demand any sort of mastery whatsoever; they just require that you do them. By virtue of doing them—even in the most mediocre fashion—you will instantly be transported to an almost elite level of performance.

Film director Woody Allen is credited with noting that "80 percent of success is showing up." In Allen's honor, we refer to these low-hanging skills as "Allenisms." If you embrace "jack of all trades and master of none" as a compliment and learn more than one of these skills—again, at which you can be entirely mediocre—you win.

The most basic and useful set of Allenisms to learn is ESP.

ESP

Potential is developing the powerful triad of experimenting, storytelling, and pitching: ESP.

All three are easy to understand and easy to do. All three should be in the tool kit of any generalist. All three require only that you bother to do them. Neither perfection nor mastery is needed!

If you develop ESP, you will have a psychic advantage over the

landlords as you will be able to better assess risk, communicate effectively, and persuade people to do your bidding.

Experimenting

In the heartwarming 1993 film *A Bronx Tale,* an Italian mobster
named Sonny helps Calogero, a young man who thinks he might be
falling in love with a girl, design an experiment to determine if she is
a keeper.

> **SONNY:** All right, listen to me. You pull up right where she is,
> right? Before you get outta the car, you lock both doors. Then,
> you get outta the car, you walk over to her. You bring her over
> to the car. You take out the key, put it in the lock, and open the
> door for her. Then you let her get in. Then you close the door
> for her. Then you walk around the back of the car and look
> through the rear window. If she doesn't reach over and lift up
> that button for you, so you can get in, dump her.

> **CALOGERO:** Just like that?

> **SONNY:** Listen to me, kid. If she doesn't reach over and lift up
> that button for you so you can get in, that means she's a selfish
> broad and all you're seeing is the tip of the iceberg. You dump
> her and you dump her fast.

Sonny's choice of experimentation in the decision-making process
is perfect. But that's not the case for most people. As we've pointed out
before, people usually tote up the perceived pros and cons of making
some decision and entirely miss any hidden salmonella or unknown
risks that might be lurking to harm them.

Let's go back to the 9-year-old you, the one who was just introduced to the scientific method. A big part of the scientific method is
the concept of experimentation.

While the thought of experimentation may conjure images of serious scientists in matching white lab coats peering into beakers atop

Bunsen burners—that couldn't be further from the truth. As done by hustlers, experimentation is the way we can predict how something works. But to make sure we're right, we set up a situation to test if something will work as we predicted.

If it works, then it strongly suggests we have a useful understanding of that thing.

If it doesn't work, or not in the way we predicted, then we don't have a good grasp about how that thing—whatever it is—works.

If we don't have a good grasp of a situation, then there's a good chance that we're about to eat hidden risk.

Wrong Risk and Binary Thinking

Our brains are designed to perceive opposites: Black and white. Good and bad. Right and wrong. On and off. Tall and short. Light and dark. Big and small. Rocky and Luke.

That's called binary thinking. Binary thinking is childish and inaccurate, and it prevents us from seeing the unseen.

Every day we're faced with on/off–type situations designed to entrap us. Take the job or leave it. Go big or go home. Now or never. Speak now or forever hold your peace.

All of these binary pairs share a common characteristic. They're all false. There is always a third, fourth, or even fourteenth way to skin a cat.

Too often, binary thinking forces us to eat the wrong kind of risk. As you learned in Chapter 2, risk isn't a bad thing—it's the type of risk and how much of it, especially hidden risk, that you want to consider.

How do we coax that hidden risk out before we take a bite? How do we see the unseen?

We test. We observe. We discover. We do this by experimenting—not in the confines of a sterile lab, but in all aspects of our lives.

N = 1

Instead of the binary all or nothing, instead of 100 percent or zero percent commitment, we can design $N = 1$ experiments. $N = 1$ is a shorthand way of saying that the number of subjects in an experiment is just one. You.

As a hustler, you're not looking for scientific certainty with your $N = 1$ experiments. You don't need random, double-blind controlled experiments to provide statistical proof of your theories.

You just need to surface risk in everyday situations.

Is that new business partner as committed as he says he is? Design an experiment that makes him show his skin in the game.

You have a new business idea. Go big or go home, amirite? Instead of mortgaging your house for the $100,000 needed to buy inventory, try buying minimal inventory and testing your ability to generate revenue.

Instead of taking the job with the crazy commute, can you contract or freelance for the same company?

Want to go gluten-free? Instead of emptying out your entire house of all gluten-contaminated foods, why not try it for a week or so and see how you feel?

Make the unknown reveal itself to you by conducting experiments in the laboratory of life.

Experiment Exercise

In what area of your life are you being offered a binary choice? Instead of accepting either choice, how can you design a test to understand the situation better?

Experimenting as part of your skill set serves another important purpose: It helps you home in on your unique path. Experimenting with side projects, with side hustles, with honeypots, with networking will be a 100x multiplier in finding your unique and oblique path.

Speaking Fluent "Eurocratese"

In 2015, Patrick found himself at the European Parliament in Brussels, Belgium, speaking on a panel about entrepreneurship in

Europe. He was next to five members of Parliament from various European countries. The moderator would ask a question—for example, "What are the structural and cultural factors holding back European entrepreneurs?"—and then go down the line to get answers from all the panelists. Then he'd start again with another question. Between the thousands of you and three of us, this is not the way to build a riveting, lively panel discussion.

Patrick happened to be last in line to provide an answer. As he listened to the other panelists fluently speak the language of European bureaucrats, the entirely unintelligible Eurocratese,* he observed that the audience was beginning to fidget and turn to their smartphones. A bit irritated that most of the audience wasn't paying any attention to him, having been bludgeoned to boredom by the long-winded nonanswers of the technocrats before him, Patrick decided to begin his turn with a short, 30-second story. When he did, the audience members looked up from their phones; some even smiled and laughed. By the third question, Patrick could see expectant faces waiting for his next anecdote.

And the best part: His stories weren't even particularly good.

Patrick was speaking extemporaneously because, frankly, he was intimidated by the sea of a thousand faces before him. As a result, he lost his train of thought. The stories' setups, conflicts, and payoffs weren't face-meltingly intriguing. Once, he didn't even connect the story to the point he wanted to make.

Seriously. Where were we?

Yet, almost miraculously, the stories worked. Not only did the audience perk up as they heard Patrick's ministories, but after the event, he was told multiple times that he was a marvelous public speaker and that it had been a joy to listen to him. And it was only because Patrick had bothered to do something that none of the members on the panel had attempted: tell stories.

---

* This is closely related to another language group, legalese.

Storytelling

On that panel populated by professional EU politicians—people who get paid to write and speak for a living, people who are in the businesses of persuading others to follow their prescriptions—no one aside from Patrick told a single story or gave an answer that was based in real-world, personal experience or that felt like part of a natural conversation.

Storytelling is a perfect example of an Allenism. Stories are the indisputable universal data format for humans, and we're designed to tell them and listen to them.

But for some unknown reason, storytelling isn't taught as part of the standard curriculum in American schools—which doesn't make any sense since story beats are buried in our DNA and being able to tell stories is just as useful as the three Rs: reading, writing, and arithmetic. The ability to tell your own personal story when networking— to tell a story about your goals and why others should help you achieve them—makes you real and authentic, and it creates a connection that no amount of statistics or presentation slides can match. You win by telling stories because most won't or don't. The modern business conference isn't that different from the traditional campfire: We gather to share stories and inspire others. When you tell a story, you allow your audience to wrap whatever data you are sharing around their brain. It's why we've seeded this book with stories and anecdotes: to mindmeld with you.

There are a number of methods to learn to tell stories. These are easily found via a Google search. However, our advice is that you focus on the right level of complexity.

Too little complexity and every single storytelling method appears to originate from Joseph Campbell's "Hero's Journey." Too much complexity and you are knee-deep in the subplot intricacies of sci-fi monster horror.

You need a Goldilocks approach. Not too much complexity, not too little complexity.

Our friend Dr. Nick Morgan, an author, speech coach, and body language expert, has a marvelously useful way of teaching storytelling that hits the Goldilocksian mark. Nick posits that there are only five archetypal stories that are combined and remixed into an infinite number of stories. They are:

The Quest: A special hero is called for some reason to achieve a particular difficult goal. Think Luke Skywalker in the original *Star Wars,* Anna in Disney's *Frozen,* and Harry Potter. All these characters are special and "marked" by their writers. When you're telling a Quest story, you must ask yourself, Does my audience see itself as intrinsically special? If they don't, you might be better off telling a Rags to Riches story.

Rags to Riches: Ordinary people achieve extraordinary things with a little bit of luck and timing. Rocky Balboa or the lovable ragamuffin Annie are prime examples, as are the authors of this very book.

Stranger in a Strange Land: Characters find themselves in a metaphoric "new land," where their old ways of thinking and doing are no longer relevant. They face the struggle of mastering something new or foreign and then adapting. *Planet of the Apes* is a classic example of this type of story. Many business speeches and pitches fall into this category.

Revenge Story: The protagonist aims to reestablish order and justice in an unfair world. Think every Liam Neeson movie known to man. Just kidding, just the *Taken* series.

Love Story: Two people or things meet and fall in love. Typically, they are fundamental opposites. Then they break up and one person has to work hard to win back the affections of the partner. This ranges from *Romeo and Juliet* to pretty much every buddy cop movie you have ever seen.

These are the fundamental stories we tell to inspire employees and managers. They are also the stories used to make a sale, to get a job, to write an op-ed or a press release, to win a date, to broker a deal, to deliver a speech—virtually any aspect of communication. They unite hearts and heads around your mission.

Da Vinci's Letter and the Power of Pitch

In 1476, Leonardo da Vinci left the employ and workshop of Andrea del Verrocchio, a master painter. Da Vinci had apprenticed himself to Verrocchio, and over the course of 10 years, he transformed from a talented 14-year-old student to a 24-year-old master as certified by the Guild of Saint Luke. In medieval Europe, the Guild of Saint Luke represented the interests of painters, illustrators, scriveners, and sculptors, as well as art dealers and art lovers. Through his apprenticeship with the multitalented Verrocchio, da Vinci became a master of more than just painting; he became familiar with mechanical and civil engineering, metalworking, sculpting, and other disciplines.

While history is unclear about da Vinci's whereabouts between 1476 and 1482, he appears to have worked on various artistic commissions for the House of Medici. At the time, the Medici family ruled the Republic of Florence, a city-state headed by Lorenzo de' Medici, known as the Magnificent.

Florence's relationships with other republics, states, and duchies on the Italian peninsula were forever tense. And none was a greater source of stress and strife than the duchy of Milan, headed by Ludovico Sforza.

For various reasons on which the historical record is ambiguous, da Vinci left Florence to find his fortune in Milan in 1482. When Medici heard that da Vinci was leaving Florence for Milan, he commissioned da Vinci to gift Sforza a silver lyre shaped like a horse's head.* The gift

---

* A handheld, U-shaped harp.

was meant to help maintain peace and good relations between the city-states.

When da Vinci arrived at Sforza's court in Milan, he not only presented the lyre but also an intriguing letter. The letter's content has been preserved and consists of an introduction, 10 points, and a conclusion. The letter's introduction serves one purpose: to give Sforza a reason to keep reading.

After the introduction, da Vinci went on to claim that he had surveyed the weapons and warmaking machines of Florence and found them lacking in unique technology. Da Vinci outlined his own skill in building physical bridges; tunneling under walls when under siege; manufacturing firearms, mortars, and bombs; designing chariots; contriving a variety of catapults; and designing buildings.

The 10 points all speak pithily to the actual and concrete problems that Sforza, as the head of state, had at the time. He was constantly fending off attackers or bringing neighboring kingdoms to heel.

Da Vinci's superlative skills and talent in painting and sculpture were left for the bottom, in a quick mention the equivalent of a post-script. "I can carry out sculpture in marble, bronze, or clay, and also in painting whatever may be done, and as well as any other, be he whom he may."

What's so marvelous about da Vinci's letter to Sforza is that it was a carefully crafted pitch. Most people, historians included, don't realize that da Vinci was equally as masterful in pitching rich, powerful patrons as he was in painting the *Mona Lisa*. His willingness to pitch played no small part in his success (as it does in the careers of all great artists).

This was a pitch designed to meet Sforza's needs, not da Vinci's. Today, more than 500 years later, many of us implicitly resist pitching. We're too good, too smart to pitch. We expect that others should see and respect our intrinsic value automatically. To pitch, we believe, is undignified groveling. In reality, pitching forces us to view ourselves from others' points of view, and it helps us build bridges from people and opportunities to our hustle.

So if Leonardo da Vinci, a singularly endowed talent, the greatest genius to ever walk the face of this Earth—easily the "smartest guy in the room" in any room he ever walked into (and those rooms weren't populated by intellectual slouches, either)—wasn't above pitching, what's stopping you?

Persuasion

Whether you call it sales or rhetoric, it doesn't matter. Persuasion is about how you pitch something: An idea. A project. A purchase. A date. Yourself as a solid investment. This is the most basic unit of commerce. It's how you present something that you want in a way that makes others want it, too. Learning even just a few of the basic techniques of persuasion will catapult you forward because most everyone else won't or doesn't take the time. It's exactly how we take more swings.

Back in the days of Patrick's youth, when he was a lowly Excel monkey (*read:* financial analyst), he once approached his boss with an idea to use technology to improve productivity.

The conversation went something along these lines.

PATRICK: So, I figured out how to solve the waiting-forever-to-load-and-save-the-workbook problem. We just need to write a macro to do the analysis.

Boss: What problem? What's a macro?

PATRICK: I already have a working prototype I slapped together, but this would be a piece of cake for a Visual Basic programmer. No more than $800.

Boss: What's Visual Basic?

PATRICK: You know, a scripting language for Excel and Word.

Boss: What's a scripting language?

PATRICK: Like a programming language. It takes routine logical tasks and makes a program out of them. This way we don't have to take coffee breaks while we're waiting for the Excel workbook to open, and there will be zero errors when we run the analysis.

Boss: Isn't that what you're supposed to be doing?

That awkward conversation can be categorized in many different ways, but one way it can't be categorized is as a pitch.

Looking back, Patrick made several mistakes, and his most critical mistake was not keeping any of his boss's needs or problems in mind when proposing this idea. Making his boss feel stupid didn't help matters, either.

This is how most employees try to persuade their bosses to take action. They ignore their boss's interests and pains and make it all about themselves. Pathetic, right?

You'd be better served just slamming your head into a brick wall. That would probably hurt less, and you'd save the embarrassment.

To give this pitch a good probability of being accepted, Patrick should have framed his own problem (a poorly designed Excel workbook that took a long time to load) in the context of a problem that his boss felt (meeting internal deadlines or getting home to see his family earlier). That's it.

Let's go back in time and hand Patrick this book to read. Now, what would his pitch sound like?

Patrick: So, I figured out how to make sure we hit all the client deadlines ahead of schedule, get you home to see your boys sooner, and keep our CEO out of your office.

Boss: Yeah? How's that?

Patrick: A lot of time we get slowed down by the software. We actually work faster than it can save and replicate the data. So we sit around waiting for it. And sometimes we miss deadlines. But there's a way to speed it up.

Boss: I'm listening. Continue.

Patrick: Microsoft designed a program for cases just like this, where Excel is being pushed to its limits. I checked with our

IT guy, and he said it wouldn't be any problem for him. If you allow for $800 in the budget, I can buy it, get it installed, and our CEO won't ambush you in the office anymore.

Boss: At lunch on Friday, grab the IT guy and walk me through how we do this.

Voilà! You now know 97 percent of what you need to know to pitch anything to anyone.

Sure, there is nuance, body language, and all sorts of psychological tricks and hacks one also uses when pitching—and you could spend a lifetime learning them. But you don't have to. For now, you just have to pitch. Pitch poorly, pitch well, it doesn't matter.

Just Pitch It

For some people, pitching is inherently discomforting. It amplifies their personal insecurities and makes them feel vulnerable. Pitching will do that to you. That's the hormetic part. But trust us on this, pitching is some of the most fun you can have with your clothes on.

It's all about getting a feeling for what the other party wants, coming up with the right ways to hook them, and then making the ask. Neil has always loved pitching, and truth be told, he has always been good at it. Patrick and Jonas came to learn the fun of pitching later on in their lives, only to discover they had latent better-than-average skills of persuasion.

If you start experimenting, start telling stories, and start pitching, you will close the gap between what you are and what you will be, and you will do it without massive risk or huge investment.

II

PEOPLE MAKE YOUR HUSTLE WHOLE

"Doing nothing for others is the undoing of ourselves."

—Horace Mann

How to Not Make Friends and Not Influence People

Ever network at an event explicitly designed for "networking"? Sporting HELLO, I'M _____ badges, and armed with our most plastic smiles and a fistful of freshly printed business cards, like bees we begin to swarm around one other.

"Where are the best-looking flowers?"

"Who has what I need?"

That guy in the charcoal suit with the maddeningly good hair, he's just gotta be someone important. Just look at all those people gathered around him.

As we slink in his direction, we think to ourselves, How do I make him like me? Can he offer me a job?

When an opening ensues, we busy-bee networkers press an unwanted business card into his hands and close with a forced smile and clumsy handshake.

And with haste, we move onto the next seemingly high-status person.

"What do you do? What's your title? What's your role?"

Whoops! She's not a VP! She's just an analyst.

Crap! We spin on our heels and abort the mission. Is it too late to ask for that tastefully thick and subtle off-white business card back?

Time to take a break as a wallflower and hide behind a glass of boxed wine.

And so it goes, people circling one another, hours wasted, cheap wine quaffed by the gallon, and bulk cheese on chintzy toothpicks consumed by the truckload. Lots of self-conscious posturing but not a single transaction closed or meaningful relationship built.

A few days later, hallelujah! We somehow do end up on the phone with someone we met, and we end up trying to sell each other on some unwelcome product or service. You ever have a conversation that went like this?

"Look, Bill, it is a fact. Your dog really does need term life insurance."

"You know, Phyllis, I'll consider the dog life insurance after you've given me that job selling dog life insurance."

Networking events end up being attended exclusively by short-sighted people who have no interest in adding to anyone else's life, desperately looking for favors from other shortsighted people who have no interest in adding to anyone else's life, desperately looking for favors . . . You get the point.

Tertius Gaudens

Welcome to how 98.1 percent of the world tacitly networks. In the academic literature, this sort of mind-set is referred to as a *tertius gaudens* orientation. *Tertius gaudens* is Latin for "the third who enjoys." In the case of social networking, tertius gaudens (TG) enjoys exploiting structural holes in networks, typically by playing two parties against one another. If you've ever met a middleman who has offered to introduce you to someone else as long as you kick back a piece of the deal (he's made the same deal to the person he's going to introduce you to), you've met a TG. The TG benefits directly from the gap in your and the other party's knowledge—and when the TG helps close that gap for you, again, they directly benefit—otherwise, they wouldn't close that gap.

Now, there are times and industries when TG mind-sets make complete sense and, in fact, increase economic welfare for all involved. And TGs seem to make a sort of natural sense as far as an older definition of hustle might suggest. But today's hustlers are tasked with taking an indirect path that implicitly involves personal innovation, manufacturing luck, and surfacing unseen opportunities. This is a radically different orientation than hoping against hope that you're able to press your card into the right hand and get a call back or serve as an unwanted middleman between two strangers.

The Greatest and Most Often Taken for Granted Opportunity

What you know; your credibility, expertise, and validity; and your level of influence (perceived or real) are undoubtedly massively important. But more important still are the people in your community, those who make up your network: your coworkers, bosses, employees, friends, and, of course, your family. These people represent the sum total of your personal and professional contacts. As Reid Hoffman and Ben Casnocha point out in their excellent career book *The Start-Up of You,* "People are opportunities. People are jobs. People are companies." People are your life. Not technology, not art, not commerce. Everything begins and ends with your relationships.

It is people who make up the second piece of your Personal Opportunity Portfolio. And it is in people that we see the most exciting place to build opportunity for the rest of your life. People are the bridge to your future, the brokers of your fate, and the faces of customers, clients, and companies. Without people, whether friends, acquaintances, or strangers, you stand relatively zero chance at success.

So if people are not your thing, it's time to rethink your social equation. And that's what we'll now help you do.

Keep in mind, the first precept of the People Piece is, unsurprisingly, that you need people and they need you. You need people to make a living. You need people in your life to advise, counsel, commune, console, guide, mentor, share, and teach. And, conversely, they need *you* in their lives for the same reasons, to help them make sense of their world, and to lead them away from the dangers of isolation, which hinder opportunity more than anything else.

People need each other not just in a loose, online, casual, on occasion, social media type of way. We need each other in a meaningful, richly rewarding, involved and engaged, personal way that weaves both the virtual interaction with the real-world meet-up-for-a-cup-of-coffee one. Ever heard the expressions "Your network is your net worth" or "No one achieves alone"? They're both true. As the work of Abraham Maslow and other psychologists has historically outlined, a sense of belonging and connectedness is one of our key drivers in life, and group belonging is paramount to your ability to build relationships, trust, and faith in fellow humanity.

Tertius Iungens

Unseen opportunity in networking means connecting with people and connecting people with each other. It requires a longer time horizon, but it takes only a simple mind-set switch: the switch to *tertius iungens* (TI), "the third who joins."

Tertius iungens is a concept coined and explored by Dr. David Obstfeld, whose research suggests that while TGs function as brokers who enjoy the fruits of connecting two parties only when profits are imminent, TIs play a longer game, "connecting people in one's social network by either introducing disconnected individuals or facilitating new coordination between connected individuals."[1]

Think of TGs as middlemen who benefit from a disunion strategy and TIs as mavens who benefit from a union strategy, especially (and paradoxically) when benefits aren't concrete or immediate.

Obstfeld's original research on TIs explored innovation in the manufacture of cars and various methods used by automobile design engineers in traversing the internal social networks at an automobile manufacturer. Obstfeld found strong evidence that a TI orientation is a predictor of involvement in successful innovation in the firm. And he suggests that TIs benefit in indirect ways from creating connections.

One of the most basic premises of TGs is that once a TG introduces two disconnected parties, the TG's advantage disappears. With this in mind, the strategy of the TI may seem self-sacrificial, but this isn't the case, because TIs create benefits indirectly over a longer period of time. After introducing two unconnected parties, the TI gains access to other parts of each party's network and can help connect further down the networks, increasing the size of the TI's own network. With the relinquishing of control (unlike a TG) comes potential for longer-term coordination, creation, and exploitation of previously unseen opportunities. In fact, as the world gets smaller and more networked together, the more you contribute to the network vis-à-vis a TI orientation, the more connected to the flows of opportunity you become.

TI IRL

When networking, instead of approaching a person while asking yourself, "What's in it for me?" approach them with the goal of expressing clearly and quickly what's in it for *them*.

In the real world, this usually falls into one of five categories.

- Acquiring new business/sales opportunities
- Maintaining client relationships
- Finding a new employer
- Hiring for a job
- Curating professional gossip and news

Opportunity Architecture Means Building Bridges

In a world populated almost entirely by TGs, where everyone else is looking out for themselves and naturally holds their interests above all else, it is imperative that you learn the TI way of connecting with people. This is the only way to separate yourself from the herd, to create value in a vacuum, and to see hidden opportunity.

First, when you begin an interaction with a stranger, focus on their interests, their fears, and their challenges. For the moment, forget about what you need. People love talking about themselves—present company included—and when we do, hustlers will perceive the beginning of opportunity as a bridge emerges between two strangers. The bridge is made up of common experiences and interests. The best hustlers can build bridges with people from any social class, profession, or interest. So as you go into a conversation, allow the other person to talk about their interests and needs.

As this mutual bridge emerges, what do your heart and your intuition tell you about the other person's needs?

Right here is where most people go wrong. Most people disposed to being friendly will have pleasant cocktail-hour conversation with someone, learn a bit about their needs, and go on to do . . . absolutely nothing.

Why would they? If I just met John, and John needed a job as a designer—well, off the top of my head, I don't know anyone who is hiring designers. Plus, I just met this guy. Who knows if he's worth spending time with?

So, good luck, John! Ciao!

What a waste of an opportunity. Luckily for us, David Obstfeld created an orientation scale that captures one's predisposition for a TI mind-set and helps us help others.

1. I introduce people to each other who might have a common strategic work interest.
2. I will try to describe an issue in a way that will appeal to a diverse set of interests.

3. I see opportunities for collaboration between people.

4. I point out the common ground shared by people who have different perspectives on an issue.

5. I introduce two people when I think they might benefit from becoming acquainted.

6. I forge connections between different people dealing with a particular issue.

Thinking across that scale—how could you help John? Aside from introducing John to someone hiring designers, you now have six ways you might be able to build a bridge to help John. These are six ways you could demonstrate and prove value to John and anyone you might connect him to—six ways you yourself can gain.

Homework: Helping Others Help Themselves

Once you've built a bridge between you and someone you've just met, the next step is homework. Not homework for you, homework for them.

Take John. John is looking for a job. You don't know of anyone actively hiring, but your online network is vast and impossible to keep tabs on 100 percent of the time. It's time you gave John some homework. Invite him to connect with you on LinkedIn and suggest that he scan your contacts for possible introductions you could make on his behalf.

Don't worry, you haven't obligated yourself to anything more than a LinkedIn addition. The next step depends on John doing his homework successfully. If he really does want a job, he'll add you and studiously review your contacts. At this point, he'll reach out to you for an introduction to Larry, Curly, and Moe. If he hasn't already provided a reason for why it is in Larry's, Curly's, and Moe's interest to connect with him—ask him to do so.

With that in hand, forward Larry, Curly, and Moe that reason and ask them if they would like an introduction. If they agree, make the introduction. If they pass, let John know they passed.

Your social capital has now increased as a result of a few simple targeted connections.

John is grateful that you took action on his behalf. Who knows, maybe you'll be asking him for the same favor in a few years.

Larry, Curly, and Moe are grateful that you keep them in mind when coming across job seekers. They know that talent is hard to find, and you have acted as a de facto talent screen. While John may or may not get hired, people are always looking to talk to and meet good people.

Honeypots, Not Boring Platforms

The allure of honey is its seductive quality. If you've ever read a Winnie the Pooh story, the poor bear will stop at no lengths to secure himself a taste of honey. Winnie is like most people who desire something, whether it's information, products, or a person's talents: If they can see the honey in the distance, they'll pursue it no matter the costs. This is why you should pull, not push, your audience, prospect, or partner.

You don't build a honeypot by being a bee. The secret is to build the hive. Get the bees to help you gather the honey. Instead of trying to be the bee that pollinates a thousand flowers, why not be the object that attracts bees from near and far?

Before Neil's blog, Quicksprout.com, became wildly popular, he knew the secret to seducing regular visitors was to share great stories and growth-hacking experiments, even if they failed. More important, by responding to people directly in his blog comments and giving valuable marketing advice for free, he made every visit a worthwhile, sticky experience.

Gil Roth works by day in an unglamorous role as president of a pharmaceutical trade association. It's a respectable position, but Gil lives a double life. He is a great lover of books and reading, and he was craving an outlet for that side of himself. No job description existed for the honeypot he desired, so he saw the unseen opportunity and felt a need to create an experience for other people just like him. What did he do? He created a podcast that he called *The Virtual Memories Show*. He reached out to famous authors and artists, interviewed them, published the interviews, and built momentum to keep going.

The writers whom he interviews get the attention they deserve, the listeners get insight into their books, and Gil builds a honeypot doing something that moves him, and by keeping his head up and eyes open for refreshing ideas and conversation. The podcast is Gil's honeypot, tapping into that which he loves: writers and the work he enjoys reading.

Gil's story teaches us valuable lessons about building honeypots. They require small doses of pain. For Gil, this meant nothing more than an investment of time and existing tools. His biggest risk? Rejection. What resources and tools do you have at your disposal now? Use those, not the tools you need tomorrow.

Gil sealed the deal to make it real. Anyone can do this; it's the classic Simple to Understand, Hard to Do type of hustle.

All Sorts of Honeypots

Instead of remaining the networking bee, flitting from flower to flower, take the time to create your own honeypot.

Honeypots can and do take all sorts of forms. They can be podcasts, blogs, conferences, meet-up groups—Patrick led a meet-up group of 3,000 technology entrepreneurs in Los Angeles. Through this meet-up, he was able to forge connections with an elite group of contacts.

Honeypots are a natural extension of TI-based networking. Anyone creating a honeypot is forced to consider what's in it for others. Why would someone else be interested in my honeypot?

The value in a honeypot is that of the work done to bridge gaps like a TI. You bridge enough gaps and people will come to you.

From Honeypot to Community

If you're lucky, your lil' honeypot will transform into a full-fledged and full-blown community. A honeypot that is no longer dependent on you is officially a community.

Communities are the people or groups of our peers with whom we share values, knowledge, and experiences in the real and online worlds. They're the friends, fans, and followers who put faith and trust in you, and you offer them the same support in return. They're the people with whom you attend events like South by Southwest, the 99U Conference, the World Domination Summit, CreativeMornings, CrossFit, and so forth. And they're the people who run in similar circles online, who enjoy learning about topics that are also of interest to you, who read blogs on, say, crowdfunding, or listen to podcasts on ways to biohack your health or improve your productivity.

Our community can include a range of people, from novices to experts. What you want is to find a broad range of talented, open, supportive, and flexible people with whom you share a common set of beliefs and values. You should be able to feel comfortable interacting with all people in this piece of your POP. So develop familiarity and ease into relationships. Always begin by collaborating and offering help. Patrick meets with a group of like-minded entrepreneurs every other Friday at 7:00 a.m. He does this to exchange ideas and develop camaraderie, and, of course, to surface opportunity. Find ways to ask, "How can I help you?" or "Is there anything I can do for you?" when in conversation with people. Most of the time the answer will be no, but the point is that you should go out of your way to gently remind people that you are there to support them in whatever form is comfortable for you. And they will reciprocate, because unless you're dealing with a sociopath or narcissist, as human beings we are hardwired to help others. It gives us a sense of purpose and makes us feel worthy.

Lucking Out at 30,000 Feet

A couple of summers back, Jonas flew to San Francisco to meet with one of his business partners, a filmmaker and producer from Costa Rica who had recently wrapped up postproduction on a movie. The two were headed to the West Coast to meet with the film's distribution team, negotiate a marketing budget, if there even was one, and detail other fund-raising efforts to raise awareness of the project. It would be a slog, and they'd need to be very creative and persuasive to get better support for the project.

As overdoers are prone to do, Jonas had worked late into the evening the night before. Sleep deprived, he boarded the plane in the morning feeling overtired and irritable.

And it got worse. For his connecting flight, he arrived at his supposed aisle seat to discover it was instead a middle seat, uncomfortably sandwiched between two other guys. There was a square-jawed linebacker type in the aisle seat, already fast asleep and blocking his entry. Jonas's arrival left the guy in the window seat uncomfortably shoehorned against the window, with less room to stretch out now that the middle seat was occupied.

Welcome to the other side of hustle: travel hell.

After a smooth takeoff, Jonas did his best to settle into a presleep position and, breathing deeply, was seconds away from drifting into dreamland when he heard a voice coming from the window seat. "Hey, I'm Dave. I'm a comedian. I live in Dallas. Nice to meet you. We're headed out to do a show on the West Coast. How 'bout you?"

As per standard protocol when one feels half-asleep, Jonas went into automatic mode. "Oh, hey. I'm Jonas. Good to meet you. Austin's my base. I'm a writer/producer, and I work on books, creative media, and film projects. I'm headed out to meet a partner and work on marketing strategy for a doc film that's releasing in a few months."

Dave remarked, "Cool. We love film. We've acted in a few movies and done a ton of commercials. You know, we have this beautiful theater in Fort Worth that seats more than 200 people. If you'd ever like to do a screening there, you're welcome anytime."

Dave continued, "By the way, we're working on a book. It would be great to get your perspective on it."

Jonas responded, "Thanks for the offer. The theater sounds

interesting. Let's figure out what we can do in the spring. And I'd be happy to read and give you some advice on your book. Send it to me."

And . . . just like that, something out of nothing. Connection. Momentum. Exhilaration!

For the next 3 hours, Dave, Jonas, and Frank, whom Dave had nudged awake, went on to have a fascinating conversation about everything from comedy, books, business, travel, and family to their goals in the coming months and a mutual desire for growth and fulfillment. None of this would have been possible had the three not been open to a conversation about what they were excited about in work and how they might help each other in life.

Two years later, Jonas has maintained a great partnership with Dave and Frank, and he's helped their team direct their growth. In turn, not only is he getting compensated for his services, he's learning the art of "Yes, and . . .," which has, in many ways, created more opportunity and led to more conversations with interesting and wildly successful people, including a few billionaires and cattle barons.

A twist of fate and a simple, unexpected conversation about shared experiences was all it took. And here's the kicker, as Dave later revealed to Jonas: "I'm on a plane 3 to 4 days a week, 48 weeks a year. Ninety-seven out of 100 times I say hello to whoever is seated next to me and conk out. Meeting you was a gift. You really opened our eyes."

One conversation. Two new contacts. Business partners for years. Friends for life. *That* is what *helping and hustling* are all about.

Before you go, we have a few tips.

People-Leverage: It's a crazy thought, but someone else is likely better than you at something. And that's okay. Here's why. You can apply the 10-Minute Rule to decide whether you have the expertise to solve a particular problem alone *or* if you must find someone else to assist you. In a way, this is how you can compress the supposed 10,000-

Hour Rule into . . . get this, a 10-minute decision. Who knew?

If you don't have the expertise required, find someone else who does. If you're looking for a software designer, you don't need to hire the next Bill Gates. You can likely find a crack coder with a few years of Ruby on Rails to handle what you need. They just need to be hungry, talented, and willing to work within your budget. Most important, they'll save you from spending 10,000 hours learning graphic design.

ABCs: The key for strengthening your ties with people is to Always Be Collaborating/Connecting. That is, you want to strive for collaboration, give and take. Instead of rushing in, look for ways to work progressively with others on your goals and projects *and* theirs as well. Define some wins you can create together over a few months. Make them manageable, and keep a list of your desired outcomes. Be sure to clarify and convey those to your collaborators for any conversations or opportunities that may arise. From coauthoring a white paper to doing an art installation, from developing an online venture to initiating something new at the office, the options are limitless, and you can build a hell of a lot of momentum by exploring collaborative work. Your energy is limited, so be sure to focus it on building together, establishing mutual support, and striving for growth. Otherwise it's likely not worth doing. As for connecting, make it a daily practice.

Uniting the Hustle Tribe

Do you need a force multiplier for when you feel like you're running out of time? Are you stuck on a problem that you cannot wrap an answer around? Unite the tribe. Showing a problem to a team of hustlers is like showing a tennis ball to a dog. Instead of dwelling on your problem, huck it out in front of your tribe. Sit back and watch them fight over the tennis ball and who can bring back the best solution. Just as dogs find tennis balls irresistible, hustlers find solving problems equally irresistible. The tribe is there to help you succeed. And you're there to help them succeed.

The focal point of any people development you do with respect to your network, honeypot, and community is to help, serve, contribute, and lead. You help by responding, giving advice, providing expertise, and making others feel good through your quirks, ideas, wit, and personality. Remember, you lead by *giving* first and receiving in response. And your interactions may not always be balanced. In fact, they rarely will be. But that doesn't mean you change. You want opportunity and you need to give before you get.

We equate strong, cultivated relationships in your POP to mightily flowing rivers with seemingly no beginning or end. The current flows in the direction of either giving or taking, of exchanging knowledge, information, experiences, expertise, and values. These yield mutual benefits and big rewards for you and your community—and often generate opportunities in the form of projects.

12

PROJECTS MAKE YOU STRONGER

"First we make our projects, then our projects make us."
—Anonymous

Making sure nothing was lost in translation was a big job for little Fran Hauser.

While other 10-year-old children were pitching fits about whether or not their peanut butter and jelly sandwiches had the crusts cut off, Fran was pitching bids for her family's masonry business.

Her father was an immigrant from Italy, a skilled stonemason who spoke broken English, at best. To put bread on the family table, her father had to understand exactly what his clients wanted done and when and where the next project would occur. When the foreman called to discuss the details of the next project, her father would motion to her to pick up the other line so she could take careful notes of the call.

To get paid on time, she was obligated to ensure that clients were clear in their requirements and, equally important, that they wouldn't take advantage of her father's English. This meant standing by her hardworking father as he negotiated fair rates for his labor. It meant giving careful driving directions to her father so he'd arrive on time at the work site—anything to help him avoid the embarrassment of getting lost or the loss of work.

Even as an elementary schoolchild, Fran was the indisputable keystone to keeping the family business running smoothly.

As she grew, so did her responsibilities as she began handling invoicing. This familiarized her with the accounting and operational side of business, skills she'd later put to use in her adult career. In the meantime, her outsized contribution helped ensure that the lights stayed on at home—and that delicious, home-cooked Italian food made it to the family table.

Together, Fran and her parents worked hard to make the family businesses successful, and they pushed forward to own their dream and build a life for their family.

Fran's entrepreneurial exposure came early and it left an imprint on her. And from these experiences, she not only developed a lifelong appreciation of her parents' Outside/Upside Hustle, she came to look at her own career from the standpoint of a stonemason. She would focus on building a firm foundation around her talents and skills, and then build creative opportunities on top of them through projects that fed her imagination, fueled her sense of fulfillment, and moved her forward toward the person she would become.

Fran's career adventure began on the Outside/Inside Hustle path from college into a major accounting firm, PricewaterhouseCoopers. She made a series of sequential Inside/Upside Hustle moves from there, surfacing her talents and honing her skills along the way. She then navigated through the competitive corporate ranks at Coca-Cola, before she was recruited away from traditional corporate ranks for a senior leadership role at upstart Moviefone and had an opportunity to rapidly improve the company's operations. In short order, she did just that, growing it into a $400 million acquisition by AOL.

With the experience of the successful deal behind her, what we call *Proof*, she again moved into a new role as vice president and general manager at AOL Movies. And when AOL later merged into Time

Warner, Fran transitioned into yet another new role, this time running the digital side of Time's Style and Entertainment Group, reconceiving and redirecting the rapid growth of Time's online assets, such as People.com and InStyle.com.

As a leader hungry for new ideas, Fran pushed for innovation at Time by applying an entrepreneurial lens *inside* the company. One project involved building a sales team to collaborate with her internal group of talented marketing and content contributors to create a more appealing online user experience.

Fran also looked *outside* the company, seeking partnerships with smaller, nimbler companies as well. She began mentoring these companies, and she took special interest in working with young female entrepreneurs. Since she was already helping these entrepreneurs, she decided to take small doses of risk by investing her own money in a number of their start-up ventures, thus putting "skin in the game" of venture capital.

Eventually, after a decade at Time's digital group, she made the shift to a new career as a venture capitalist and joined upstart Rothenberg Ventures, where she continues to invest in and develop emerging start-ups with deep promise.

Fran doesn't see her career like most people might. She doesn't see a continuous line of jobs. Rather, she sees her work as a sequence of investment bets, parts of a broader *portfolio of projects,* and a basket of assets that provides her upside optionality and diversifies her overall risk.

She's not afraid to pursue new opportunities, and she intuitively understands that a rich, integrated, and creative life is based not on doing the same one job but on constantly stretching and surfacing her talents through new endeavors. Thus, she maximizes her hustle through her many projects—one at a time—and lowers her risk exposure. If any one venture, project, or endeavor stalls or fails, Fran has wisely made other well-placed bets that might bring a windfall of money, meaning, and momentum.

Viewed over the course of 25 years, Fran's adventure appears punctuated not by jobs but by projects. And this series has allowed her to build a POP to succeed in unexpected and life-enhancing ways.

This is what a steady hustle does for you: Before you know it, it stacks the deck—and the odds for success—in your favor to create a dream career you can happily own. And your stacked deck of projects ultimately becomes your legacy. Now that's something worth hustling toward.

Projects, Not Careers, Are the Foundation of Your Hustle

Unless you've been locked away in a cubicle inside a cave in the far reaches of Siberia, you know full well that the meaning of *career* has changed dramatically. No longer do we expect or are we expected to stay in any one type of role or any one type of company for any enduring period. Like it or not, technology, globalization, and the evolution of work have obliterated the old model.

The new, new, and new you dictates a heart, head, and habits for a different hustle. This hustle is defined by a project-based career orientation and will no doubt utilize your talents and empower you in new ways, many of them unseen and unexploited by you currently.

Let us briefly look at how we arrived here. The 1950s and 1960s were mostly a boom time of growth and stability. You had, say, one job and one company only. You had a loyal, long, and dedicated career, one which culminated 40 years later in a retirement party and a watch or a pendant. Stability made sense for the time, and for the old dream.

The 1960s became the 1970s, and that one company and one job became maybe two companies, but still with one main profession. If you were a journalist, you were still a journalist, but maybe you hopped outlets, from newspaper A to newspaper B or magazine C.

More upheaval hit in the late 1970s and 1980s. Technology moved rapidly, and tough times indicated the path had changed. Along came the 1990s, the Internet, exuberance, and a rock 'n' roll president who played the saxophone. You got hired by a tech company, working on content for its website, until you hopped at the chance to join a start-up in Seattle because the company's value proposition and growth prospects looked appealing. And the dream had shifted.

Suddenly, people at all levels today find their security slipping away, their backup plans gone, and an army of young, hungry upstarts willing to work for free doing the jobs that people used to make a living on. On the other hand, there is *more* freelance and project-based work than ever before through an infinite number of outlets that can be cobbled together into a fabulous lifestyle within the control of the worker, who can suddenly choose assignments, work the hours she chooses, and use her home as an office with a freedom that workers have never before enjoyed. Sound like hustle?

The point of the above soliloquy is that times have changed, sped up, and evolved so rapidly that the exalted 1950s ideal of one career with one company in one lifetime has gone the way of the dodo. So instead of worrying about this radical reorientation of our professional reality, the way we want you to think of your career, even if you find yourself in a role at a stable company, a rare gift, is to plan for the path of multiple minicareers at best, or even, dare we say, an "uncareer." This is the project-oriented way of work, and this shift toward it, the way of hustle.

This idea is especially important if you're an aspiring entrepreneur or a self-declared nonconformist who doesn't fit or envision fitting into a traditional role anyway. If you do opt for a traditional role, our advice still holds true—you can protect yourself against downside risk by constantly pursuing stimulating projects (a portfolio) that provide additional income and opportunity. And if you're a knowledge or creative worker, you're going to do projects—dozens of them in any year, and hundreds of them throughout your lifetime! These will give shape to your professional identity, and they'll also shape your sense of purpose and meaning—much more than any one particular job title or role might.

The Project Economy:
Observing the Way of Work for Hustlers

If you want to know where the hustle class of people like us—we mean creative people who show up each day to cheat the odds, challenge convention, and change the world in ways both small and big— are today and will be tomorrow, keep your head up and eyes open. Stroll on down to your local coffee shop, aka coworking space, aka remote office, aka "the cloud." Once there, pick up a tasty beverage of your choosing and take a look around you. What do you see?

On this day, to our left sits an attractive food blogger who's working on her novel. At a table across from us, we greet a salt-and-pepper-haired executive in conversation with a venture capitalist we pitched to a few months ago for feedback about an idea for a start-up. A couple slips by, exiting the café: She's an architect working on a new commercial building, and her partner is a financial consultant who splits her time between here and Shanghai. Over in the corner we notice a brightly dressed designer who has an office a few blocks away. She's fleshing out UX comps for a real estate company's mobile app.

And, of course, there's an advertising agency team, consisting of an account executive, a writer, and a creative director, meeting with their client, in from New Jersey. Oh, and then there's the contracts lawyer—he's working on a nondisclosure agreement issue with his friend, a health care professional who was formerly an army nurse overseas but has transitioned into entrepreneurship with a killer new concept for delivering low-cost mobile medicine to the masses.

Still in line stands a city administrator; followed by a substitute teacher who's a gifted singer with a YouTube channel through which she offers voice lessons; and an Uber or Lyft driver, not sure which he prefers, frankly, who's also a talented trumpeter with a gig tomorrow night. There are still others, like the tattoo artist who owns a vegan food truck, and the hairstylist who's also a photographer, whom we don't recognize today because of her blue hairdo.

We're surrounded, swimming in a sea of hungry dreamers and doers, driven by an unquenchable thirst to push forward. All of them not choosing careers, per se, but instead *doing projects that move them.*

Each one of these folks feels certain of one thing: What they're doing at this moment, while creative and fulfilling, *may not* be the same exact gig they'll be doing at this time next year or the year after. They work intensely and apply the best of their talents and focus to any project—and they work to define their lives in the space between working to live and living to work.

Like all members of the Hustle Generation, they're upbeat and optimistic. Their toil enables them to actively bring in decent money, with the promise of them doing a lot of interesting work and, if necessary, carrying several job titles simultaneously. They're okay with that reality.

The other part that's clear is that the vast majority of these folks *do not* self-identify as careerists, nor do they aspire to any one specific title. They don't self-describe through a particular job, either. They're self-motivated to develop real POP, and they're dynamic because they have no choice but to continually seek new opportunity.

And, frankly, they wouldn't have it any other way.

Welcome to the project economy. It's a place where getting paid to make things happen comes first, and job titles are secondary, if necessary at all.

In any modern city across the country and around the globe, you can take stock of scenes like this. They help us connect dots around the shifting tides of labor, of caffeinated creative juices a-flowing, of individual curiosities meeting demand in the marketplace. And they give us a strong sense of how jobs and work itself are being reinvented, and where the broader economy, or at least your place in it, looks headed. You can also understand how smart companies seek to stay ahead of this curve, looking to fit into the creative matrix of collaborative, cloud-, and project-based work today.

Project Buckets

When thinking about your own means of generating money, meaning, and momentum, it's helpful to break your life's work—your daily, weekly, monthly, and yearly output—into project buckets. Into these project buckets you'll place your time, talents, and skills; your capabilities and creativity; your priorities; and any new opportunity that arises, so bring your A-game and get ready to swing.

Hustling is intended to enable you to bring your best work into the world. It's about choosing projects that move you forward and allowing yourself to execute at a high level. This is why getting this piece of POP right pushes plan A (your dream) closer to reality and helps you get beyond the doldrums of plan B (any filler work you take on in the meantime).

Three Types of Projects

1. Day Job (Ongoing, the "Nine-to-Five")

Commonly, the day job is what many mistakenly think of as the totality of their career, the coveted title or position they're working toward or worked so hard to secure. *It's not.* It's a day job, or if you work at night, it's a night job. It can change quickly. In other words, it's simply your most regular means of income. It's not permanent, and only the naïve view it as such. Sorry. However, it is, at least temporarily, the firm foundation upon which you sustain yourself. It's your chief means of income and often the biggest energetic focus for you. For most working in corporate jobs, this is where you make your primary contribution day to day and month to month. And the same is true if you're working for yourself. The day job may feel fixed, but it should be thought of as a fluid adventure.

There of course are exceptions. If you're like our friend Amit, an executive at PayPal with a long track record of success at Dell and other huge companies, this is a position you're likely going to keep for a while. You're leading a team within a leading company. If the role stimulates you, affords you growth opportunities and areas in which you can innovate, and pays you well, it makes sense to keep it. Or if you're already well on your entrepreneurial journey, doing the Outside/Upside Hustle, like Wendy, who went from raising her kids as a stay-at-home mom to a seven-figure-income-earning real estate agent and investor in a couple of years, then by all means, don't quit your day job!

2. Experiments and Side Projects (Part-Time, the "Five-to-Nine")

As you know from reading about the Potential Piece in Chapter 10, experiments are a way to regularly take small risks and try to find new ways to solve problems or come up with novel solutions. They allow you to quickly push your boundaries around pain and gain, winning, losing, and learning. And they afford you the ability to test, observe, and measure outcomes.

Neil is a world-class experimenter, and he has documented his exploits on his blog. He'll run numerous experiments in a single day, from A/B testing e-mails and landing pages to ensure optimal click-through and conversion results to driving online-traffic-generation campaigns. He even ran an experiment wherein he bought many tens of thousands of dollars' worth of clothes and measured how they helped him attract new relationships. For one, he met several NBA players who commented on his $3,000 sweatshirt. His new clothes attracted new business, too. When Neil shifted his appearance from casual to more of a classy sartorial elegance, the new wardrobe awarded him with rich consulting opportunities from entrepreneurs who were attracted to his dapper look. The point is, Neil experiments with a purpose or outcome goal in mind. If it's buying outrageously expensive clothes, he'll aim to earn a handsome return or relationships on the investment, while knowing he'd prefer to do other things than shop and is normally a low-key polo-shirt-and-jeans kind of guy. You can experiment, too, and it helps to be clear about your objectives and open to possible outcomes.

FIVE SIMPLE EXPERIMENTS

1. **Experiment with your e-mail length.** Test the impact of using only one-sentence e-mails for one week. Does it hurt or help your time and your relationships? Ask for feedback.

2. **Experiment with your vocabulary.** Make it purely positive and optimistic. Test neurolinguistic programming (NLP) terms every day for 2 weeks straight. Measure the impact in how you feel, observe whether others respond to you any differently, and note if you're more or less productive.

3. **Experiment with your sleep hours.** Test if sleeping 1 more hour per day for a week adversely or positively impacts you. If nothing else, it will force you into a more regular sleep schedule.

4. **Experiment with your work hours.** Test if reducing your time required in the office by 1 hour less a week adversely or positively impacts you. Get permission from your manager first, if need be.

5. **Experiment with your exercise regimen.** Test the benefits of running in short sprints rather than long jogs or exercising intensely in small bursts for a few minutes every other day. If yoga is your preference, try a more intense, shorter flow of asanas for 1 full week. Then double the amount of time. Note how it impacts your mood and your energy level.

Side projects differ from experiments. They are commonly referred to as gigs, if you're an artist or musician, or side hustles if you're a consultant, copywriter, designer, dog walker, eBay merchant, marketer, programmer, part-time day trader, ride-sharing-service driver, part-time real estate agent, or Airbnb host. The point is, side projects involve the things you do *aside* from your day job, and they're not typically full-time endeavors. They allow you to earn extra income, surface your talents, and explore your curiosity or creativity in ways your day job doesn't. Usually, side projects require a bit more of a sustained commitment than experiments, and they can include both online and offline work.

FIVE SIMPLE SIDE PROJECTS

1. Write an e-book

2. Open an e-commerce store on Amazon, eBay, or Etsy

3. Become an online coach or tutor

4. Develop an online course

5. Host an Airbnb, if it's allowed in your home

3. Value-Add Projects (Extra Time/Weekends/Leisure)

There's a key difference between value-add projects and the day job or side project buckets. Value adding means pursuing areas of interest that do not necessarily fill your financial coffers but instead fill your creative, educational, spiritual, and experiential meaning coffers. Such projects can be richly rewarding. Often, these take the form of volunteer work or apprenticeships.

It's not easy to get paid to do what you love. This is especially true if you're a creatively inclined person with undeveloped or underdeveloped talents (think of Patrick with his guitar).

But it's easy to pay to take a class or to find ways to apprentice or volunteer with an expert. So value-add projects offer a way to rapidly equip yourself with knowledge, give yourself experiences, and unlock talents. One value-add project could be apprenticing for a seasoned local photographer to learn how to deal with lighting and composition in your digital photos so they draw more attention and likes on Instagram. Or maybe you want to learn how to become a cabinetmaker and know an exceptional local carpenter. Trading a few hours a week at the carpenter's studio sweeping up or helping out could do you some good.

Value-add projects can also be a means to give back to the

community in some way, such as by helping out at a nonprofit. Maybe you could donate a few hours at a homeless shelter or soup kitchen 1 day a month or work with children at a foster care or mentoring program or give time to help out at a local animal rescue or adoption facility. When your day job and side project are not doing the job to fulfill your need to give back, you must do something else that moves you closer to a place of meaning. And that's a key void that value-add projects can fill. Find a way to trade your time and talents for small doses of life experience that you just can't get nor fulfill through your usual means of work.

FIVE SIMPLE VALUE-ADD PROJECTS

1. Apprentice with an expert in an area of interest—digital photography, carpentry, gardening, filmmaking, painting, music, and so forth.

2. Volunteer at a nonprofit for a cause that's deeply important to you.

3. Give your time to a group in your community who can benefit from your existing expertise.

4. Ask for a non-job-related assignment at your day job that would allow you to explore a new role or do research in a new area.

5. Create a local club for social good. Pick one thing to do each month and work together to make a small difference in your community. It could be cleaning up a park or painting a mural in an approved public space.

Projects Lead to Proof

Projects are about how you shape your present life and work. They are the creative way you propel yourself forward into the next leg of your life's journey. And, move over Hamburger Helper, projects are also a huge hormetic aid: The more difficult the problem, the more varied the work, the more complex the requirement, the stronger the project will make you.

Doing the same types of tasks over and over might have been okay 10 years ago. Today it puts you at great risk; it makes you a one-hit wonder, an overly specialized pony. *Someone utterly replaceable.* And worse, sameness and routine stifle your ability to respond to a changing work environment and fluid job market. They can lead to a deep sense of meh and never point you down the path to discovering your true talents.

The Projects Piece makes us stronger, as we continually stretch our skill set and test our mettle in new and challenging contexts, as we solve problems and find out what results we can produce and what we can deliver to others in terms of value in the market.

The point of the Projects Piece is to continue to find your hidden talents and to put yourself in a position to thrive by staying in motion. The more options for upside or opportunities for growth, the better. The more you can try new ways to build money, meaning, and momentum, the more you'll learn about how wonderfully expansive your creativity and capabilities are.

Projects Are Productions

Every project worth doing, whether it's designing and programming a mobile gaming app, writing an e-book, launching a food truck business, painting a landscape, doing a photography shoot, planning an event, or you name it, has its own rhythm. Many projects require a set of experts, and you get to decide who these people are and how many, if any, you will need. Projects also follow a creative and execution process that needs to be well conceived, planned, organized, and managed efficiently.

From 10,000 feet up, the process looks like a few moving pieces arranged in an order.

1. You name your project.

2. You clarify a goal.

3. You set a deadline.

4. You figure out a list of collaborators.

5. You determine the pieces. What work needs to be done?

6. You assign. Who will do which parts?

7. You prioritize. Which pieces come first?

8. You execute. You solve a problem through creative means. And you measure results against expectations.

Actually, the one thing that matters most as a producer is step 8—that you execute. That you fulfill your promises and get 'er done. You execute on time and on budget, and you measure the quality of your work and your experience to determine how you might improve future projects.

So in truth, it looks more like this step alone.

8. You execute. You solve a problem through creative means. And you measure results against expectations.

So whether it's for your day job, where you're making a presentation to your team, an experiment or side project to deliver copy for a new e-commerce website to a customer, or value-add work like editing a short film for a friend, you want, above all, to make a commitment to execute and "just do it." Put simply, you'll go a long way toward creating value and positive, shared experiences when you solve problems and help others succeed. The cumulative effect of successful projects, and their visible imprint, is what we call Proof, which we flesh out in the next chapter.

From Hustler to Creative Producer

As Fran Hauser's story illustrates, she's not simply an accountant who's doing business. She's a doer and a leader who understands the value of being able to excel in multiple roles, as well as where to find (and how to direct) talented people to tackle challenging tasks and solve problems creatively. While her title says something different, Fran acts as a *creative producer* not just to further her own projects and pursuits, but also to further those of the people she mentors.

Creativity requires risk taking and small doses of pain to solve problems in novel ways. As does *producing* a work, or bringing a project to the finish line. Hence, for anyone who hustles, "creative producer" is a title you want to strive toward. Here's why: Jobs (the way we work) and companies (the context in which we work) are really just large-scale creative projects requiring a person who can shift roles quickly, display talents across those roles, and execute to produce a desired outcome. As we mentioned in Chapter 3, hyperspecialization is best left to insects. You want to creatively produce desired outcomes by thinking *and* doing things in unique and oblique ways.

Now you may know someone who is the type of person we call a hybrid person. In fact, you may be one of them. You might be the experience seeker who enjoys design work as much as you like blogging about the New York Knicks. You lead a rich, unusually varied, broad life driven by ideas and entrepreneurial or artistic projects through which you tackle problems you can solve.

Next, you'll learn more about what becoming a better doer signals to the universe.

13

PROOF MAKES YOU BULLETPROOF

> "... and when is enough proof enough?"
> —Jonathan Safran Foer, *Everything Is Illuminated*

Ah, opportunity, sweet opportunity. Bedrock of the American Dream. What a mystical, majestic, delicious, omnipresent, addictive, and elusive thing you are.

Nothing, and we mean nothing, rings truer of freedom than opportunity. And there's nothing more American than the pursuit of opportunity—it's one of our most deeply held ideals and among the chief reasons we consider our friends in the Hustle Generation an optimistic lot.

In point of fact, it's one of the very reasons we wrote this book. *We love opportunity.* But some opportunities don't love us; they are more challenging to chase than others that seem to fall into our hands. And sometimes, well, you just need to create your own opportunity.

This is precisely what an enterprising young professional named

Nina sought to do. She looked to get a foot in the door at Airbnb head-quarters, the start-up unicorn of her professional affection. Having built and sold her previous company in the Middle East, Nina felt drawn to the opportunity, sophisticated problem solving, and global community building she could do in Silicon Valley.

She applauded the "making something out of nothing" and hustle mentality of successful start-ups and high-tech companies. And she wanted to build anew and root herself at the epicenter of 21st-century world change and transformative economic possibility.

Though her contacts there were few, she moved to San Francisco with the confidence of knowing she had already developed a success-ful company that had grown to 52 colleagues. Now it was time to explore stimulating tech companies and the novelty of what looked like fulfilling work opportunities. Nina followed the rules and did the sort of blocking and tackling we all expect to do when seeking employ-ment: She did her research on companies, tailored her résumé, wrote letters, and applied to dozens upon dozens of jobs.

And then she waited . . . and hoped.

A year later, she was still waiting for an offer she could accept. And then her eureka moment struck. It dawned on Nina that she didn't have to play by the regular rules of applying for a job she wanted—nudging, poking, hoping, and waiting for a response that *might* hopefully lead to an interview. Or it might lead nowhere. Instead, she thought, she could reverse engineer a more favorable set of circumstances, much like the path we covered in Chapter 7, where you start at point B (in Nina's case, getting hired into the position she wanted) and work backward to point A (the entry appli-cation point to the keys to the kingdom of Airbnb, Nina's preferred company).

Nina set out to do just that. First, she targeted Airbnb and learned all she could about its brand, its growth strategy, its leader-ship, its culture, and more. She distilled exactly the type of roles that she believed best suited her skills, talents, and experience (a mix of marketing, operations, business development, and coffeemaking). And then she got more creative. Working with a designer, she designed and developed a custom website that *resembled* an actual Airbnb profile page, with the domain nina4airbnb.com.

From there, she went a layer of proof deeper, immersing herself in geographic and psychographic user research. She studied data and trends on Middle East population growth and desirable locations. She identified places where Airbnb might prosper by setting up new host sites, driving traction into cities like Dubai and expanding the brand and community footprint in an underserved growth market.

The proof didn't stop there either. Nina wrote a white paper laying out the data points, strategy, and economic opportunity for Airbnb. She defined what growth in a new market could look like, in which cities, and more. And, finally, when the dots had connected, she launched the site, leveraging her expertise in online marketing and social media. Nina reached out to her e-mail list to announce the new site and her findings and simply asked her network to spread word if they found the white paper—and her approach—appealing.

She activated her social influencers, who in turn chatted her up to key decision makers at Airbnb, including one of its founders and, separately, a recruiting director. Queen Rania of Jordan, a customer of Nina's previous business, jumped on the bandwagon, urging Airbnb to interview Nina. And from there, Nina's unconventional résumé and innovative approach got her even more momentum. Her hard proof led to a foot in the door at Airbnb, which led to an interview there and, beyond that, inquiries from literally thousands of other companies around the globe. Nina's confidence, momentum, and ingenuity created a seismic ripple of attraction, a magnet that herds of recruiters couldn't resist. In the end, it was they, not her, who chased after the trophy.

Eventually, after much publicity and social media fist-bumping, Nina had an intriguing problem: She was flooded with more job offers than she could process. In an ironic twist, offers flowed in from amazing companies doing interesting work around the globe. After considering all of her newfound options, she chose to accept a position at, get this, not Airbnb but Upwork, a dynamic company that pairs talented freelance workers with those looking to hire them for projects. There Nina enjoys building community around the world, doing satisfying work, and making a meaningful contribution that moves her forward daily. Nina's quest had taken an unexpected turn and led her in a forward but different direction. Her new point B looked vastly different from the destination she'd aimed for initially. That's the beauty of obliquity. And the power of creating a unique, differentiated, and original proof of concept.

Nina's boldness liberated her from the pitfalls of the average job market and the formulaic following of the rules that leaves so many people waiting indefinitely for a chance at a job they will likely never get. Rules, as anyone who hustles knows, are often capricious and antiquated. They form arbitrary hamster wheels, which hinder our ability to get ahead. Nina created proof to position herself for success, and her success became a celebrated and thoroughly impressive reworking of the rules of workplace hiring. Her story shows that you need not always play by the rules of the system. Nina innovated by starting—and winning—the game in her own value-add way.*

Alchemy and Icebergs

As we quest for more, we work through the fourth piece of POP and recognize that creating proof means going beyond the normal representations of all you've done professionally, creatively, and "otherwisely." Proof is allowing others to *experience your abilities of creation* directly: not simply via the words in a résumé, but by being able to interact with your creation at some sensory level, hence being able to appreciate your creative abilities.

---

* To learn more about Nina's story, visit nina4airbnb.com.

The Truth about Proof

Here's an example of how proof works. Neil and Patrick have to make a decision to hire one of two software engineers.

Bill is the absolute best programmer in the world in Assembly, but he has no open-source projects available.

Viola is pretty good at programming in Assembly, and she has multiple open-source projects and apps available for download.

There would be no question about it. Neil and Patrick would hire Viola in a heartbeat. Not only can they experience Viola's work directly, but they also know that Viola understands and appreciates the alchemy of multidisciplinary work, under the surface, and that is required in the creation of anything from an ancient temple to a software app to this book.

This book is, literally, 65,000+ words strung together, but if you think that a book is about writing words, you'd be wrong.

Cranking out words is probably the least important aspect of book creation—other aspects include marketing; designing the cover; experimenting with ideas; developing good, conceptual hooks; balancing the needs of your agent, your coauthors, your editors and publisher—the list could go on and on.

All of these happen under the surface, and when they are dealt with, a book—that is, more than just 65,000+ words—is produced as proof. That's how alchemy happens.

Proof represents the perfect remedy for righting the wrongs of an imperfect talent-recruiting system. Your proof is the absolute separator, the line in the sand, the pieces visible and invisible, inspirational and explainable, the breakthrough work that you are offering to the world as opposed to the other people vying for the same position.

Whether it's applying for a new job, capturing the interest of a would-be business partner, or even drawing the attention of a lover, proof provides concrete inarguable evidence that you are unique. It is that which sets you apart from the herd.

Proof, in many respects, is just the tip of the iceberg of what

PROOF	LACK OF PROOF
Iceberg (most of it below the surface)	Ice Floe (nothing below the surface)
Alchemy $2 + 2 = 5$	Ordinary $2 + 2 = 4$
Others experience directly	Others read or hear about
Strong signal	Weak signal
Hustle habit	Conventional thinking
Self-directed	Needs direction
Active	Passive
3-D	2-D

you're capable of. Proof can be the obvious work you've done in the past that's clearly observable, be it online or verifiable via references. This kind of proof floats on the surface of the sea. Anyone will notice it jutting out among the smaller ice floes, the piles of competitors' résumés. Proof gives observers just a taste of what you can do, while still obscuring the many talents and skills that went into the work you've already completed.

For example, you might have built your proof into a major project that you've completed in the past. It could have been a website that you conceived, designed, and funded, and for which you hired the coders in India, managed the team of copywriters, and collaborated with SEO and marketing folks to hack into a strong search ranking in a competitive space. Or, let's say it's a lauded event you planned, programmed, and publicized for the past few years that brought in a million dollars for a childhood literacy nonprofit. People who hire you want to know you've achieved results, but they also need to know your capability and the invisible work or job descriptions that you can fulfill, like all the heroic, albeit uncelebrated, tasks you drive and slogging you do on projects. Your proof can be the beginning and sometimes, like in Nina's case, a strong conversation that speaks to your abilities and value proposition—the big magic you bring to the table for any would-be recruiter, client, customer, or business partner.

Résumés Really Are for Dinosaurs

Kelly O'Mara is a former recruiting executive who worked in the Enterprise and Cloud Services Division of Google. Today she runs Shynebyte, her own recruiting boutique in New York. We spoke with her about the challenges of today's job market. On the one hand, qualified job applicants are desperately looking to stand out in a crowded and competitive high-tech market. On the other hand, companies face a difficult burden when recruiting talent. There's a lot of talent out there, but there's also a lot of not-so-great talent gunning for the same positions. As digital tools have made it easier to separate the wheat from the chaff, the amount of chaff has exponentially increased.

Kelly shared with us the reality that the average résumé gets reviewed for a total of, get this, 6 seconds. Think about that for a moment. All those hours of work you've invested into creating a tailored masterpiece for that coveted job will earn you 6 seconds of human résumé review, if it gets reviewed at all. And how many people do you know, yourself included, perhaps, who have applied for numerous in-demand positions and not heard a peep back? Likely many. A lack of POP is part of the problem. With such an overwhelming number of résumés to sift through, companies need motivated applicants to go above and beyond to stand out.

For many companies, large, medium, and small, the applicant-recruiting program presents real challenges. Human resources may be understaffed, may lack the tools required to efficiently assess quality applicants, may simply have too many qualified applicants, or may be plagued by poor job descriptions and ineffective hiring criteria sets, to name just some of the potential problems. It's a broken system for a variety of reasons.

So what does this mean for you, the seeker? It means wide-open opportunity to do something unexpected and remarkable through your proof and your hustle. In other words, in looking for the job you want, you'll need to "go and show." You'll need to go well beyond the résumé *and* show proof of your talents and skills by doing something exceptional, unique, and, preferably, share-worthy on social media.

The point is, take more risk. Be adventurous, bold, and creative. You never know what kind of luck it might yield.

From Icebergs to Proofbergs

If you're a normal person, you likely don't boast multicolored peacock feathers to spread open and share with the world on demand; nor would you want to dress up as a wild animal to call attention to yourself. Not only would an act like that be hard to maintain, but it might draw you some odd looks, too. So ditch the animal suit and let's help you prop up your POP through proof and use better ways to help decision makers and people of influence find and identify you as indispensable talent. There are ways to show, indisputably, that you are worthy of curiosity, conversation, and much more—that *you* are the proven person who can deliver the goods.

Going beyond or navigating around the usual rules might make you feel awkward, give you a sense of pause, or even cause cognitive dissonance and visceral discomfort. That's expected at first, as you dislodge from the lie that the right way to get ahead is to patiently wait in line. The old rules of success don't work anymore. There are too many people vying for too few positions, and it's up to you to create the momentum that ensures that you are one of the few getting ahead.

In Chapter 3, we described job descriptions as icebergs. Most of what is important is underneath the surface. When it comes to selling ourselves, we must invert that knowledge and attract opportunity—we must bring what is underneath the surface to the top. We must build a "Proofberg."

Your Proofberg is the unseen or hidden block of the proof that, like the iceberg, offers something deeper. Visible proof (a website, a film, a white paper, a new app) alone can't possibly reflect the hours and energy exerted in thinking and doing, pushing and pulling a project forward. The Proofberg shows proof of concept that you've gone well beyond a normal job description to get a project done. If proof is the ultimate evidence of tangible and intangible value creation, your Proofberg speaks to your willingness to do the impossible, to build projects, products, or intellectual property most will never do.

So, when it comes to your next job application, you might best be served by rethinking your approach. Instead of spending hours tailoring your résumé, draw out the Proof Piece: How can others directly experience proof of your ability to create?

Begin there and work on novel and respectful approaches that will get you noticed by the company you wish to work for or opportunity you wish to pursue. Don't settle for going from point A to point B when point B might not ever present itself as an option. Instead, work out the reverse path and look for ways to leverage your talents and skills, be disruptive, and stand out. May the résumé-application-alone approach forever rest in peace.

Proof Is Show Don't Tell

In Hollywood, Bollywood, and Chollywood, as well as other major film-production hubs around the globe, stories are told primarily through movies—moving pictures. The operating code is *"show* don't *tell,"* and visual language reigns supreme. At the same time, in our courts of law, the burden of proof often falls to the presentation of concrete evidence. A picture can say a thousand words, so much of our human experience is hardwired through images. The point is, we use proof, visible and tangible, as a means of defining an experience or outcome. And that's true, too, when it comes to POP and our expression of identity.

The Proof Piece in POP runs deep and is central to our ability to hustle. It points the people with opportunities to dole out specifically to a place where they can find out more about our endeavors and exploits, our values and adventures.

Some of the key attributes of the Proof Piece include:

- **Discoverability:** Are you "searchable"? Can you be found online? If you Google or Bing your name, you should instantly have the gratification of seeing your identity and pursuits reflected in the search engine results. You're "somebody," and the search will show these results to anyone curious enough to know who you really are. They might see your online profile on popular social media platforms like Twitter or LinkedIn, in any media coverage you've garnered, and so forth. The key here is to ensure the results are an authentic expression of you, and preferably not damning, maligning, or inaccurate in any way. It should go without saying, but not only should you be easily discoverable with a quick online search, but what people are finding out about you should be positive in tone and make you look good. Scratch that, it should make you look great. Invest the time in creating a better website with high-quality photos and mentions of you. Sound basic? It is. But many don't bother.

- **Experiential Markers:** These include the work you've completed, even as a hobby, such as making an image gallery for your photography or creating a YouTube channel with video you've shot on weekends or while traveling and edited to demonstrate your storytelling technique or commanding presence on camera. It could also be a blog that you've developed or links that lead to posts you've contributed to prominent sites with tons of traffic. It might be an award-winning design project you art directed. Or it could be an example of social good, such as a richly rewarding cause that you've supported, like ending homelessness, for which your efforts for driving awareness or directing fundraising can be displayed.

- **Positioning/Image/Story:** This is the way you personally define yourself across virtual and real-world channels; it's how you present yourself to the world. Examples include the biography on your site, your social media handles and feeds, and your profile photos. These form the core pieces of your story and influence how you are viewed by others. So be sure to work through your story and read it aloud; share it with a couple of trusted confidants before you share it with the world. And be sure to update your bio at least once per year. You're constantly growing, and your bio should reflect that growth, even if it's merely adding a sentence about a new endeavor or learning you've done.

- **Quirky Luck:** These are the unique markers or identifiers that set you apart from others and frame your unique experience. Often, your quirks are the noticeable differentiators in how you present yourself. Quirks can be quite attractive to employers and lovers, so you must take them very seriously. They are often attributes with which people identify you. For example, Neil's quirks include his unassuming, down-to-earth presence. He's approachable, authentic, disarming, funny, and—stop us from further flattery—immediately likable. Those quirks are visible online and in the real world, and they produce tremendous luck for Neil as he hustles through work and life. Further, Neil's popular blog and media coverage position him to win. They show he's a leading expert on, to name a few things, speaking on business matters, online marketing, and real-world entrepreneurship. If you don't believe me, just Google him. That's proof positive this piece matters.

- **Track Record:** Your proof speaks to your performance, and often when you send someone to your website, they'll look for evidence that encapsulates a few positive aspects of your journey. You can show this through a past win, such as an award or recognition of sorts. Your proof validates you and gives you instant credibility in the eyes of others. Maybe you can offer a photo of your family, your children, or something you're particularly proud of. Proof can also come in the form of a testimonial or quote from a person of influence, or from your online connections, friends, and followers. In his seminal work *Influence: Science and Practice,* psychologist Robert Cialdini defined this as "social proof," where your trustworthiness and importance are a direct product of your perception in the online world. Finally, proof expresses what you've done and why it matters. For example, Patrick's audio-technology company, Superpowered, offers Android developers a lightning-fast, low-latency mobile audio experience. While it's a niche software, people recognize the quality and proof that he and his team have created.

Proof, restated, is the seen and unseen creativity, initiative, skills, and talents you possess. For your Proof Piece, the most important thing you can do is offer a way for people to find you—and find you interesting. This is important for prospective employers, business partners, customers, new contacts, or even a person who might be a future date. The two basic necessities are an online presence, like a website revealing an interesting aspect of your being, preferably a blog that runs on WordPress or an aesthetically pleasing site offered by Squarespace, and a social media presence that is well maintained and moderately active, with a post at least once or twice a week (even the busiest neo-Luddite can handle that challenge).

Lastly, never forget the importance of keeping your Proofberg looking well cared for and deliberately well tended.

The Moment of Proof

Nirvan Mullick knows a thing or two about the multiple benefits of proof.

As a 1996 Toyota Corolla–driving freelance experimental artist and filmmaker based in Los Angeles, at 37 years old, Nirvan stumbled onto a proof-making experiment when he was headed deep into East Los Angeles, hunting for a used car part. A door handle, to be precise.

Passing up several car garages and colorful auto outfitters, he found the store of George Monroy, a hardworking auto parts seller whose shop was barely eking out an existence. As George searched for Nirvan's prized Corolla part, Nirvan was approached by George's then 9-year-old son, Caine.

Caine had taken on the unique project of building an imitation "state-of-the-art" arcade, fashioned completely out of car parts, cardboard boxes, and plastic toys.

Sadly, Caine hadn't found much reception in terms of players and customers. But Nirvan, with the eye of an artist, saw something unseen. Like a 37-year-old kid in a candy shop, he indulged Caine by buying $2 worth of tickets for pretend-play at the cardboard arcade.

Floored by Caine's creativity, Nirvan played a number of games and, afterward, asked George if he could make Caine the subject of his next short film.

George agreed, and the manufacture of luck began. Nirvan set up a Facebook event and organized a flash mob to be in the film. Nirvan filmed *Caine's Arcade* as a 10-minute documentary aimed to showcase one child's remarkable imagination and habit of creation. A few months later, he posted the film to YouTube, not suspecting an unusual reception.

Oh, Nirvan had one other ask of viewers and fans: He sought financial donations via social media for Caine's college fund. He pressed his friends and followers with a question: "If he could do this with a cardboard box, imagine what Caine could do with an engineering degree?"

Hundreds of thousands of dollars later, and with more than 5 million views on YouTube, Nirvan's short film had gone viral, hitting the front page of Reddit and getting picked up by a number of major media news outlets. Actor Jack Black brought his children to the arcade to play. At times, the line at the arcade swelled to 4 hours long. Caine became a celebrity of sorts, and a movement around imagination was unleashed.

This oblique, unique discovery, as a result of Nirvan's search for a car part, turned into a source of inspiration and affection for *millions of people* around the world. Justin Timberlake called Caine his "new favorite entrepreneur."

Caine and Nirvan had a defining moment, where Caine's star was born and Nirvan's ascended. Nirvan's proof was epic, and proof positive that "a small gesture can change the life of a child." And, at the same time, it can change the life of a struggling filmmaker, too.

The donations, which continued to pour in, and the curiosity around Caine led Nirvan to launch a nonprofit to "find, foster, and fund creativity and entrepreneurship in kids like Caine." He called it the Imagination Foundation.

Nirvan took a swing through a creative project—an experiment in doing something that moved him. It not only established his proof but rewrote his future.

Due in part to the short film's massive success, Nirvan is well on his way to owning his dreams. Beyond launching his successful nonprofit, he continues speaking around the world on storytelling, creativity, and the power of imagination. He works with youth on large-scale projects with major support from foundations. He has development deals with HBO, Disney, and other studios and continues doing his film work.

Nirvan ran with a moving idea: Caine was the embodiment of not what our world is, but of what it *could be* for children—a place of fun, intelligence, imagination, entrepreneurship, and shared experience. Because he kept his head up and eyes open, Nirvan created a one-of-a-kind story of his own making and let momentum carry him the rest of the way.

14

MONEY: THE MEANS OF MOMENTUM

"What would have become of us if Kahnweiler hadn't had a business sense?"

—Pablo Picasso

In the waning days of World War II, Pablo Picasso entertained an old friend and colleague, a photographer named Brassaï, at his studio in Paris. The pair had met years prior when Brassaï had been commissioned to photograph Picasso's sculpture work.

This visit, as recorded by Brassaï, was informal. Previously, Brassaï had mentioned to Picasso that he had given the arts of illustration and freehand drawing a try as a young man, and Picasso wanted to see some of Brassaï's youthful attempts. On this visit, Brassaï showed Picasso his drawings, now 2 decades old, and Picasso remarked that Brassaï had talent worth pursuing and recommended that he hold an exhibition to sell his drawings.

By this time, Brassaï was already well known as a photographer, having built a successful career during the interwar period chronicling

Parisian people and places with his iconic black-and-white images, many of which you have no doubt seen. (If not, Google his work.)

The insecure Brassaï responded to Picasso that he did not have enough talent in the art of drawing, and that only a fraction of artists have enough talent to be financially successful.

Picasso proceeded to enlighten Brassaï on the importance of money. "Well, success is an important thing!" said Picasso. "It's often been said that an artist ought to work for himself, for the 'love of art,' that he ought to have contempt for success. Untrue!"

Let's leave Pablo's words hanging in the air and travel through time and space from 1944 to 1816, to Lake Geneva, Switzerland. There, a coterie of daring Romantic artists led by writers Lord Byron and Percy Bysshe Shelley gathered on the Swiss-French border to take in the sun-drenched scenery and progressive political climate.

The group sought a form of aesthetic purity and perpetuated the idea that suffering, whether psychic, spiritual, physical, or other, was *necessary* to make meaning, or "moral excellence."

We can thank these Romantics for today's commonly held belief, which Hugh McLeod reiterates in his otherwise refreshing book *Ignore Everybody: And 39 Other Keys to Creativity,* that "art suffers the moment other people start paying for it," and that money perverts meaning, purpose, and our higher selves. In art, suffering has an intrinsic value as a cathartic process by which one attains a certain moral purity untainted by the lewdness of material needs.

"Art for art's sake," they tell us. "Never compromise your art." And, worst of all, "Don't sell out."

But it is not just the artists among us who suffer from hang-ups about money and its evils. The fact is, most of us do. We've seen our friends and colleagues say one thing and then do an entirely different thing. They complain ceaselessly about their bosses but refuse to find a new job. They come up with a great idea for a product or service and talk about it endlessly but take zero steps to make it real. They self-sabotage around money.

We could have just as easily included another *p* word in the POP component of your hustle: *profit.* You should *always* look to profit from your work. When you can profit monetarily, even if it's a small profit, that monetary gain is what you need and want to sustain your hustle. If you have the blessings of being a world-class artistic prodigy like Picasso, or you're working your way to becoming a late-blooming bestselling mega-author like James Patterson (or like your authors, for that matter), or you're someone just starting to explore your own creative adventure in the form of side projects, your hustle needs to lead with profit.

Alternatively, if you're making a career move, an Inside/Outside Hustle like transitioning from a full-time role in a company to a free-lancing role, then steady profit is the bridge that helps move you from merely surviving to positively thriving. It expands your capacity to fulfill your potential. You already know that you can provide value to others. The key is knowing what that value (your time and talent, i.e., your work) is worth to others, what they'll pay you for it, and then making it a habit to ask for more—do not settle for anything less than that amount. The mantra to breathe in is this: Price is only an issue in the absence of value. If your asking price is right, so too will be your profit.

Thus, profit to sustain your momentum is absolutely, fundamentally, positively critical. As Picasso told Brassaï, "An artist needs success. And not only to live off it, but especially to produce his body of work."

The myths around money and meaning, around money and art, have survived for too long. It's time to shut these down and rewire any remaining skepticism. We want you to be hungry for the right reasons, never the wrong ones.

Starve Your Starving Artist, Feed Your Hungry Hustler

Ironically, the myth of the starving artist contemptuous of material success has created more bad art than the influence of money ever has. It's high time we starved him out of your consciousness.

It is not money but, rather, a *lack* of money that compromises art.

Make no mistake, Picasso's early artistic and, paramount, *financial* success is what allowed him to remain uncompromising in his art and his career—a career defined as the greatest of any visual artist of the 20th century, providing us with meaningful explorations and expressions in new modes and original forms.

We don't expect you to carry the burden of the prodigious talent like Picasso, but we do expect you to think sensibly about the relationship between money and meaning with a little help from biochemistry.

10-Year-Old Logic

When you were 10 years old and you wanted to swim across the pool underwater, you did what every other 10-year-old did: You started hyperventilating poolside.

Your 10-year-old self figured that since fourth-grade science class had taught you that oxygen was critical to survival, and that carbon dioxide was a waste product of your lungs, the best way to increase your oxygen supply would be to breathe in a large amount of air in a short time to oxygenate your body. Now fully oxygenated, you would clearly break your big brother's backyard record of 6½ underwater back-and-forth laps.

The fact that you got a teeny bit dizzy and your parents kept a watchful eye on you was a clue: *Your 10-year-old self had it wrong.*

Wait! What in the name of art does hyperventilation have to do with money, meaning, and momentum?

Only everything.

Stop holding your breath. Breathe normally—not too deep, not too shallow—and keep reading.

Hyperventilation

Hyperventilating doesn't help increase oxygen levels in our blood. In fact, hyperventilating reduces oxygen in arterial blood.

This is because of two critical reasons: First, hemoglobin (the protein that transports oxygen from your lungs to your cells) in your blood is already 98 percent saturated with oxygen. You cannot naturally supersaturate (increase to levels above 100 percent) your blood by hyperventilating. Second, by hyperventilating, you expel carbon dioxide from your tissues into the environment, which has the unfortunate effect of making it more difficult for hemoglobin to release its oxygen payload.

Got that?

Trying to increase oxygen makes it more difficult to use oxygen, because hemoglobin needs carbon dioxide to oxygenate your tissues. Without enough carbon dioxide, the oxygen molecules remain bound to the hemoglobin protein. In short, we bet you an extralarge Slurpee and last week's allowance that you cannot make it to the far side of the pool and back all the way underwater.

The Bohr Effect

In 1904, Danish physiologist Christian Bohr clearly demonstrated that hemoglobin's oxygen-binding property is inversely related both to acidity and to the concentration of carbon dioxide. This relationship between the ratios of oxygen and carbon dioxide in blood chemistry is known as the Bohr effect.

In plain English: An increase of carbon dioxide in blood makes blood more acidic, which has the effect of hemoglobin releasing oxygen to body tissues. Remember: Ultimately, hemoglobin's job is to release the oxygen it picked up in your lungs. If it doesn't release it, then why carry it?

Without carbon dioxide, you cannot breathe. Carbon dioxide isn't a waste product; it is an important blood gas that keeps you alive. For you to keep breathing, you need both oxygen *and* carbon dioxide.

Tight Ranges

You now know the basics of blood chemistry. And yes, we hear you: We know you didn't buy this book to learn physiology and biochemistry. But hold your breath for just one more moment with us.

The relative ratios of the amounts of carbon dioxide and oxygen in your blood are vital. If you're an astronaut, a scuba diver, or a physician taking care of newborns, you know well the dangers of too much or too little of either gas being present.

We'll skip the gory details, but severe changes in the level of either gas in either direction (+/-) rapidly change your blood acidity levels (pH), and if that happens, well, terrible things are in store for you.

But not to worry, your blood acidity levels are tightly controlled by your body automatically. If you find yourself outside of the normal pH range for blood, your body will kick in to bring that level back to the tight range it needs to be in (7.35–7.45 for the bio nerds keeping track at home).

This phenomenon is known as homeostasis. The body regulates the variables that control blood pH so that blood pH remains stable and constant. If blood pH remains stable and constant, you keep on' keepin' on. You keep breathing. You keep hustling.

Too Much Money

We all know the dangers of focusing on the pursuit of money. It should go without saying that we've all felt money's corrupting influence on our lives at one time or another.

Maybe you've taken that well-paid job at the shady company with the dodgy CEO and pyramid sch—umm, questionable business model? And then hated yourself for it.

We've bought expensive clothes we didn't even like in order to impress our cool friends. We've even taken vacations at expensive and overrated places in order to check them off our bucket lists because our boss had visited the year prior or because it was where everybody else on our Facebook feed was going.

This is all completely natural, understandable, and entirely human. And of course, just like "hypercapnia," the presence of too much carbon dioxide in the blood, it's dangerous.

Too Much Meaning

Meaning. It's how we contribute to society, how we enrich others beyond the material, how we connect in a way that gives us the confidence that we matter—that our life choices matter and that we are part of a bigger picture.

We all seek it.

But perhaps we've gone too far in that direction at times, too, overdosing in our search for meaning at the expense of other important factors.

Today more than ever, we hear stories all the time of people who turn themselves inside out avoiding commercial activity and transaction because business is "gross and inhuman."

Fed up with our crappy jobs, we yearn to avoid life's irritations by retreating to a ranch in Big Sky, Montana, close to wild horses and open fields, far from the daily commute and brutal grind.

These kinds of dreams and reactions aren't wrong, necessarily, but our understanding of what is wrong usually is. Many artists and free spirits never understand that the hole they are trying to fill with too much meaning is akin to "hyperoxia." What does that mean? When you're trying to breathe, too much oxygen will effin' kill you.

Bohr Effect Meet the More Effect

It's not that money can solve all our problems, and it's not that meaning always repairs the meh in our hearts. It's that money and meaning have to be in a proportionate relationship with one another.

This is the "More effect." Just like oxygen and carbon dioxide in the Bohr effect, the relationship between money and meaning has a tight range that your unconscious constantly monitors.

Too much money relative to meaning leaves you asking yourself, Why am I doing what I do? Am I being paid off for some unconscionable act?

Too much meaning relative to money, and you ask yourself, How do I keep living this way without putting myself at risk of calamity?

Either way, if the relationship between the two is disrupted or falls out of balance, then you are out of homeostasis. Your heart will signal to your head that a return to equilibrium is needed. That signal feels a lot like the elusive "more" we seek to erase that meh in our hearts.

When money and meaning are in homeostasis, something magical occurs. In the same way that oxygen and carbon dioxide are both necessary for you to breathe without thought, money and meaning work together to create the most wonderful life force: momentum. And it is this essential force, a force for good and a force for alignment in heart, head, and habits, that leads us from subtle changes to seismic progress as we build toward an infinite hustle that has no beginning nor end.

15

DEFINITE MEANING

"The depth of learning is in direct relation to the intensity of experience."

—Robert Monroe

Last-Minute Phone Call

"Have plans tomorrow?" Paul asked.

Muting the episode of *X-Files* on the TV and shifting the phone to his left ear, Jonas replied, "Ah, you know. The usual. Work. Write. Hit the gym, teach a yoga class, and see Laura. What's up?"

"I don't think so," said Paul. "You ain't doin' none of that. You're coming to Houston."

Amused by his old friend's cheekiness, Jonas indulged him. "And why would I do that?"

"To meet the Dalai Lama." Paul insisted.

Jonas's friend was an organizer of a Houston-based Buddhist group, and that group happened to be hosting a symposium called "Spiritualism and Science in the Modern World." Designed to break the barriers between spirituality and science, the event featured a number of impressive attendees, folks like Nobel laureates, scientific pioneers,

Hollywood actors, and, of course, a stable of Tibetan Buddhist monks. It was headlined by none other than the Dalai Lama himself. Jonas's friend needed a few trusted volunteers to ensure smooth operation and had made a late-night call to Jonas in Austin, about 4 hours away by car, knowing that Jonas would find the experience fascinating.

For Jonas, a young writer deeply interested in spirituality, it was a once-in-a-lifetime opportunity, an opportunity that most in attendance were paying thousands of dollars for. That left him no choice but to take a sick day from his nine-to-five advertising job and make the drive to Houston.

Jonas figured he had a hooky day to burn, and this would be, by far, the best use of it. He would return to work the following day, so he thought, "No big deal."

No big deal, that is, until you understand the historical context. This was September 2005, a few years before we had an iPhone and up-to-the-second weather apps at the tap of a finger, and a few weeks after Hurricane Katrina had inundated New Orleans, resulting in the deaths and displacement of thousands. It was also a time when Jonas had sworn off taking in most news and media—who needs weather forecasts, after all?

After hanging up with his friend, Jonas e-mailed his boss to let her know he wouldn't be in the next day. A few fitful hours of sleep later, Jonas left Austin at 3:00 a.m. and arrived at the event in Houston 4 hours later. He was tired but excited, ready to volunteer and observe the Dalai Lama and other distinguished guests.

Various presentations followed. Some addressed seeking balance between the demands of life and the demands of the spirit. One included an explanation of quantum mechanics and unified theory. Later, a debate arose about the value of spiritual philosophy versus the absolute laws of physics. At first, the exchange of ideas was diplomatic, but the courtesy gave way to an unexpected condescension from the scientific camp. Sure, science had a firm claim on truth, but the questions posed to the Dalai Lama were taking an unkind and impolite turn. The smug contempt then turned into blatant patronizing, and the audience began to fidget uncomfortably in their seats. Jonas, for one, wasn't amused.

But as the event moved into its closing moments, the background chatter suddenly ceased as all watched the dais. His Holiness's face lit up with a wide smile, and his joy crystallized. It was easy to see that the only thing that mattered to him at that moment, the only thing that was meaningful and significant, was not the debate over truth but instead the sheer beauty of a small green ficus plant, presented as a gift from a group of Buddhist students who attended a nearby Houston university.

In that moment, egos were cast aside, all the unspoken tension dissipated, and the entire room focused on a simple act of giving and an exchange of kindness. Grins and smiles broke out in the audience. All it took was a houseplant to bring people together. Who knew?

Jonas's frustration turned into bliss. He nodded his head in appreciation and joined the crowd joyfully exiting the conference.

After hours of provocative presentations, questions left unanswered, lectures, group meditation and chanting, and a challenging Q&A, the single best experience, arguably the most poignant of the event, occurred when the Dalai Lama's charisma outshone the petty, righteous anger in the room.

If the Dalai Lama wasn't angry at being disrespected, why should Jonas be angry?

After the event, what Jonas wanted most was to get on the road back to Austin so he could have some quiet time to reflect.

And he would have more than plenty of time.

Go Due East to Get West

While the calming thoughts of the symposium's close set in, outside a storm of biblical proportions brewed: Hurricane Rita, among the most intense hurricanes ever recorded in the Atlantic, was quickly closing in on the Houston area, and evacuation orders from the city's mayor were already under way.

In a matter of hours, upward of 3 million people—families with children, families with grandparents, families with animals—hit every major inland road available in search of safety from the coming tempest. Surveying the traffic and the predicted weather patterns, Jonas hatched an unconventional plan: Instead of getting stuck in traffic at 6:00 p.m. along with everyone else, he figured the better plan would be to have an evening meal, grab a few hours of sleep in his car, and leave at 3:00 a.m. to avoid traffic and still make it back to Austin in time for work. "No big deal," he thought.

As Jonas confidently pulled onto the highway at 3:00 a.m., he met with traffic stuck at a standstill. He began to think he had made a colossal mistake. By 10:00 a.m., he was sure of it. He had made less than 7 miles of progress. Exhausted, stressed, and hot (he had turned off his AC to conserve gasoline), he questioned his plan.

Then Jonas got a call from his girlfriend—and his aunt and other family members in rapid succession—imploring him to "find gas now." His family had been following news reports about a local gasoline shortage due to the mass exodus.

Jonas had already attempted to find gas earlier, twice, but none was available, with millions of cars sucking up all available resources and no gas trucks available for several days.

Nervously, Jonas decided to take action. His gut told him that waiting out the storm in Houston was a bad idea, but he wasn't making any progress on his way to Austin, either. He pulled off the highway.

Within 1 minute of making the decision to detour from the million-car snarl on the highway, Jonas encountered a gas station with just enough gas left to fill his tank. He picked up the last Snickers bar in the minimart, an ancient bag of sour cream and onion potato chips, and a gallon of water to fill his dehydrated body.

As Jonas stretched and contemplated his next move, he noticed a sunburned firefighter in overalls sitting outside the gas station, surrounded by trash, broken-down cars, and the smell of human waste.

Jonas approached the broad-shouldered, red-bearded man and asked for directions.

"If you want to avoid the highway, there's a farm road. You'll go due east. It's straight this-a-way, and then when you hit Ranch Road—"

Jonas interrupted him. "Sir, I don't think you understand. I need to go west, to Austin, not back to Houston."

The man motioned confidently. "Turn left. Head due east. And from there you just haul ass straight on down—for about 30 miles—'til it dumps you back out on old I-10. Go east, son, if you want to get west."

And haul ass Jonas did. Due east. He didn't see a single car on the road besides his.

Not a one.

Instead, he saw cows and horses, trees and ranches, farms and fields. Most important, he had enough juice in his old-school candy bar phone to talk to friends and family who checked in on him, nudging him on, cheering him on his safe return home.

And as the long road eventually banked westward, he took in the most sensational slow-moving sunset he'd ever seen, one he would remember for the rest of his life.

In time, that worn, undulating farm road led him back to the old highway, which was moving at steady speed, and that old highway merged onto a major thoroughfare that led back to Austin.

Jonas had trouble processing the experience of those 24 hours. It had been equal parts miraculous, humiliating, enlightening, and annoying.

It was not the time at the conference, not the physicists confronting the Dalai Lama and agreeing to disagree on whether science was the absolute truth that stuck with Jonas. Rather, it was the humility and humanity of being stuck in standstill traffic for nearly 13 hours. That, and the powerful visuals: the looks of worry and exhaustion on peoples' faces and the apocalyptic scenes from the day, like the loose cattle, broken-down cars, and trash strewn across the highway. And the unspoken gifts of serendipity and survival—more than 100 people died on that same stretch of road that day, not by the Hurricane itself, but by the conditions and panic created by the evacuation.

Most important was a deep sense of gratitude that Jonas finally would get home safely and be able to get back to work the next day. And that the surprise stretch of farm road, a saving grace that led him due east to go west, underscored the oblique nature of how we move toward meaning. It's always through our own experiences, however indirect, humbling, or confusing, that we find the right path.

Making Sense of Your Quest for Meaning

No matter your preference—be it as a person of faith and spirit or science and humanity—in the quest for meaning, you have to work to discover it on your own and do the work on your own time. Meaning, whether through faith, study, or observation, becomes its own project in momentum, one that begins as we hustle toward an outcome or goal via experience, even in an indirect way.

It's this path of trial and error that leads us to reveal our own truths, in much the same way that we surface our talents. And it's also a path that not only endures but is incredibly significant to our lives, identities, and well-being. Just as we add pieces to our POP, so too must we add layers of meaning.

Our quest to experience meaning offers us significant lessons in fulfillment. First, when we pursue new experiences with energy, intention, and decisive choice, we stop asking, "What could be?" and we learn to start answering with "What is." We actively influence our destiny through the actions we take and the truths these reveal, not through hypotheticals or things we don't do. It can be said that if action—our hustle—serves as the ultimate way to make meaning, then obliquity is like the farm roads we take in our everyday life.

By choosing to go after things that move us forward, that inspire us to action, we get a glimpse of the deeper forces pulling us from within. It's these forces that we can equate to the elusive "why" we end our hustle with—the one that ties our life's purpose together from all of the disparate experiences we have over time.

You need not go crazy in your hunt for meaning nor put your life on the line to locate deeper significance. You can instead seek and find it in the everyday corners of life. Finding meaning only requires increasing your awareness, discerning what matters from what doesn't. And you don't have to go to extremes to find it.

It means not ignoring that voice within you, but instead learning to listen to yourself. And it requires you to set your ego aside at times, so you can be thankful for the chance to be alive, to hustle another day, no matter how intense the external environment might be or how tough the conditions and circumstances you're facing.

Meaning might come through curiosity and everyday interactions that lead to serendipity, and it might just hit you like a hurricane after a conference. Like with the truths and talents revealed in our hustle, you may find meaning tucked away in the hidden or unexplored areas of your life's work, the ones often left unnoticed.

Exercise: A Few Tips for Extracting More Meaning from Your Everyday

Meaning through Reciprocity: It helps to approach every situation and interaction with kindness, support, and openness, as if it will have a positive, mutually beneficial outcome for you and whoever else is involved. If someone does something on your behalf or that benefits you, return the favor. Find small ways to give back to others. Even if only a gesture, ask, "What can I do for you?"

Meaning through Reflection: Practice meditation or yoga or find quiet time for reflection and "plugging back into yourself" each day. Even 20 minutes a day of mindful breathing can have a profound impact on your mood, mind-set, and clarity. An easy way to do this is to sit and feel your breath move through your body. Let your mind unwind, Try to envision any thoughts you have like waves moving through your mind. Don't attach or react to them, just acknowledge and affirm them with a gentle, silent "yes."

Meaning through Gratitude: Go out of your way to say "Thank you" when you normally wouldn't. At work, at home, at the gym, at the café, and so forth, why not give someone a nod of thanks and a compliment? And, of course, accept compliments from others with a wide-eyed smile and a vocal "Thank you." Small acts like these go a long way.

Meaning through Relationships: Spend time with people you enjoy and broaden your social circle. Stay connected with others and involved in their lives. Send someone a short letter or send a silly post-card. Cultivate friendships with wise people significantly older than you and those younger than you. Avoid the trap of living in a closed bubble. You never know when following up with an acquaintance, new or old, could result in an incredible opportunity or meaningful life event.

Meaning through Community Experiences: People attend events like Burning Man and conferences like South by Southwest and Wisdom 2.0 to connect with other people. These events provide a way to find like-minded people, enjoy shared experiences, and make unforgettable memories. Whether it's a national forum such as those or a more local gathering, you will derive enormous meaning when you seek out your tribe and create meaning together. Create a budget and time off for these kinds of experiences. They pay spiritual dividends.

CONCLUSION

INFINITE HUSTLE

"A finite game is played for the purpose of winning, an infinite game for the purpose of continuing the play."

—James P. Carse

The End of the Beginning

Wherever you find yourself, whatever you wish to create for yourself, whatever you want to prove to the world, wherever your excitement or frustrations reside, and whether you're suffering or in bliss, if there's one thing that our life and our hustle teaches us, it is that we can *always* begin anew and continue the journey.

So in this, our concluding chapter, we celebrate the significance of continual experience, reflection, and energetic recharge in your pursuit of making momentum, money, and, ultimately, meaning.

That last part, meaning, is one we make through the hands-on direct experience of our hustle. It is only that experience that can push us toward fulfillment and a richer recognition of where we've been, the work we've done, and who we've become.

It's a scary thought for some, not knowing who we really are or where we're going. The work and life of hustle can lead us down unexpected paths and usually involves cutting some of our own, which is exciting but has an unpredictability that can sometimes be daunting. Our sense of identity feels fleeting at times, and for good reason. How we see ourselves and how the world sees us is an ever-shifting lens. Neither is fixed. But the truth is that nothing else is fixed, either: no job, no relationship, no status. Permanence is a false comfort that prevents us from aspiring to greatness. When we get to a place where we can accept the evolving nature of our identity and the significance of who and what we've become, we can draw an ineffable appreciation via reflecting on how we've spent our energy over the years, how we've used up our precious ticking time, and what we choose to do with the days ahead.

It's this reflection that yields us perspective and appreciation and that allows us to derive the elusive *more* we seek from our hustle in work and life. The potential we've fulfilled, the people we've known, the projects we've undertaken, and the validation of credibility—the proof—sustain us. The POP we develop imbues us with a sense of possibility, confidence, and love for doing what we do. And that love is a quest that begins only by beginning, by moving and by doing, by hustling to unlock the great sustaining energy of momentum as we continue pushing forward.

Thus we refer to the process as an infinite hustle, like wave after undulating wave of motion in the ocean, which makes for an experience that can't be replicated, sensed, or felt anyplace else. The real-world hustle demands the gift of presence and yields a spiritual magic—the virtual and the vicarious forms just don't cut it.

So, as we arrive at the end of the book, we remember that the only way to draw benefits from the hustle is by actually *doing* things ourselves, through taking risks, making luck, and finding opportunity in unexpected places. Only then, by *ending* rather than starting with our *why*, do we find *our* why and make authentic meaning of ourselves and our lives. Our why isn't a destination, it is, as the age-old cliché suggests, a journey. Focusing too much on self-understanding is often counterproductive, which is why the oblique method of doing is optimal. To better understand yourself, don't think. In a word, hustle.

Though we may try, as Steve Jobs eloquently put it, to "connect the dots looking forward," we know the limitations and that we "can only connect them looking backward." Connecting dots in reverse is a meditative process of reflection, one we can practice daily. And its rewards deliver personal and professional dividends, as we draw an enhanced awareness of meaning through our day-to-day choices and experiences. Our hustle remains a lifelong quest to better understand the nature of our truest selves. Staying present and mindful in the quest is the key.

Unplug the Hustler

A shift toward meaning, mindfulness, and deeper awareness of our hustle enables us to keep ourselves fresh, focused, and feeling vibrant. It forces us to put a hard stop on both our "business routine" and our "busyness routine," and it disrupts and disorients our traditional no-nonsense, nonstop hustle personality.

We recommend regular resetting with blocks of unscheduled time each week, and especially when on the periodic vacation or day off. Resets free us from the need for constant doing, which isn't really an effective way to do business or live life anyway.

So we emphasize the importance of *rethinking* schedules and working to create your *ideal unschedule*, which gives you the time required not only to allow for recharge but for surprises and serendipity as well.

Resting by Moving

The fastest way to burn out is to frenetically and frantically react to everything and anything. Experienced hustlers know that you have to rest by moving.

What this means is that you should:

1. Take time to go off the grid.
2. Make sure your vacation or sabbatical involves move-ment—at least one new experience that liberates you from preexisting experiences and stretches your senses.

It's a different way to keep up that momentum, but once you learn to hustle, you will feel rejuvenated as you move toward completely different experiences during your reset!

Gregory Berns, author of *Iconoclast: A Neuroscientist Reveals How to Think Differently,* writes, "Only when the brain is confronted with stimuli that it has not seen before, does it start to reorganize perception. The surest way to provoke the imagination, then, is to seek out environments you have no experience with." This is true even when you're on vacation—where it's more vital than ever.

Scheduling the Anti-Schedule

In work and life, perfection is never the goal, and filling all the time on your calendar isn't the goal, either. Far from it.

Too many managers, consultants, entrepreneurs, and creative workers make this mistake. In the spirit of maximizing productivity, individuals may find themselves in a state of adrenal fatigue and emotional burnout. Slowing down is a necessary benefit, and scheduling time to recover must be part of the daily regimen.

Here's a tip: Don't book all your time in your schedule. In fact, specifically block out 10 to 20 percent of your time each week for creativity. That means 4 to 8 hours a week where you can't react to other people's agendas. Taking this time will be extremely difficult at first, because conventional thinking doesn't explicitly value this sort of scheduling. Take time to revisit your ongoing self-diagnosing talent exercise.

After a few months, you'll realize this "off time" is when you've come up with some of your best ideas and learn more about your innate talents. New paths to fulfilling your potential will become clear. The anti-schedule is a reset tool, so use it wisely and you'll wonder how you ever lived any other way. As our friend and author of *Love Is the Killer App*, Tim Sanders says, "Creativity is what happens in the white spaces on our calendars."

The Difference between the Hustler and the Armchair Hustler

Most of us don't have private jets that can whisk us off to exotic locales or operate in the kind of circles where we can casually schedule private meetings with the greatest minds of our time at a moment's notice. And since that lifestyle isn't available, many people think that the next best thing is to learn about what it would feel like, to live vicariously through the words and exploits of others.

Armchair travelers read about the experience of shamanic healing rituals and the thrill of hopping on a seaplane at midnight deep in the Amazon basin of Iquitos, Brazil. They see characters weave their way through the jungle, jumping to avoid the jaws of hungry jaguars. They feel the rush of adrenaline of our fearless narrator as sweat drips from the small of her back and she breathes deeply peering out over a 2,000-foot waterfall.

But the armchair traveler knows this indirectly, second-hand at best, only in his imagination.

He doesn't *really* know the intricacies of planning the trip or the headaches of airline delays or lost luggage in foreign lands. He doesn't know the exhilarating feelings of arriving in a remote area like Maun, Botswana, deep in the Okavango Delta in the heat of the summer and not having proper gear but deciding to go out into "the bush" anyway because it's a once-in-a-lifetime chance to track wild lions and see elephants and hippos frolicking in the marsh.

Armchair chefs read cookbooks, listen to podcasts, and watch cooking programs. They see the dynamic textures and colors of intensely creative recipes. But they can't taste the exotic berries combined with fresh-from-the-farm cream and rich, rare liquor from South America that's so sweet it'd make your bone marrow dance. They can't smell the aroma from a freshly ground bag of animal-digested coffee-beans-turned-fresh-brew (sounds revolting yet it's amazing stuff) called kopi luwak, among the most exotic of joes in the world, or the buzz of drinking it before waltzing around the ruins of Angkor Wat's heart chamber. Because the armchair chef isn't really there in the flesh.

Armchair artists read about but don't do their art. Armchair entrepreneurs read about but don't do business. Armchair dreamers dream but don't own their dreams.

It might sound harsh, but it's the *doing,* the habit of the hustle, that reveals the real you that you deserve to become. Your armchair is a safety net for wishing to win but being willing to lose. The problem with armchair hustlers, or armchair anything for that matter, is that they can only know—and only grow—by direct experience. By putting themselves on the path by putting one foot in front of the other and bringing momentum to their hustle.

So by depriving yourself of the experience of doing something that moves you, by not keeping your head up and eyes open to look for opportunity, and by avoiding sealing the deal to make it real by asking and getting the transaction, closing the partnership or landing the new project or gig, you're missing out on learning about who you really are and what your true potential looks like.

In choosing to hustle, you will be astonished by how much adventure your life will be filled with and how many doors you will be able to open. It doesn't matter where your starting point is. It doesn't matter if you're a late bloomer. The most important thing is to begin today.

Your Real Why

When we started fleshing out the ideas for this book, there was one idea we all agreed upon right away. When it came to helping people own their dreams, we promised we *wouldn't* start with the why.

No one ever knows his or her why. The "why" of why you do any-thing—get married, have kids, become a doctor, direct a film, design a bridge, or even write a book—is never clear at the outset. Never. It just seems like it is.

Yes, your brain prepares socially acceptable superficial whys to explain to friends and family why you did this and why you did that. "Mommy, I want to be a doctor because I love helping people." "Guys, I want to be a management consultant because I love strategy." But this is just sand in your (and their) eyes.

And as such, the superficial why that you can verbalize blinds you and is entirely unhelpful in telling you which direction to head.

The *real* why—the one that is often hidden from you by your own heart and by your own head—your purpose, your meaning, is only ever revealed by hustling. And by failing. And by losing. And by succeeding. And by winning. And by hustling again. What we're say-ing is that your real meaning becomes clear when you simply start swinging your spiritual, energetic, and enthusiastic bat at life.

Why comes from experience. Why comes from experimenting. Why comes from doing the wrong things. Why comes from *bad decisions.* Don't get hung up on why you are doing whatever it is you are doing.

Owning Dreams Ain't an Overnight Process

If you think about it, life's hard, isn't it? Nipping at your every moment are family responsibilities, bills, and obligations. And the worries of the world, like war, terrorism, drought, and disease, occupy our airwaves.

We understand. But let's do a visualization exercise just for a moment. Let's say tomorrow morning was different. You awaken bright and early, feeling renewed and clear-minded. The world fixed itself overnight. And so did your life. You sit up in bed, and warm rays of sunlight shower your room. The birds and squirrels chirp away. You stand up to take a deep, slow breath and stretch your arms high. The sun feels great on your skin. For a moment you contemplate life. "Aaaaahhhhhhhh," you utter, exhaling, just grateful to be alive.

Relaxed, you walk into your kitchen. You smile, thinking, Why, yes, life *is* good.

And then it's time to create your first frothy, hot, caffeinated drink of the day. You sip it, feeling *even better* with each gulp. You then open the crisp, freshly delivered paper and digest the news. Guess what? *You* are the front-page story! Again.

HUSTLE READER BECOMES OVERNIGHT SUCCESS

You read further and discover that you've not only stashed away $5 million in the bank, but another $5 million is on the way. How can this be? Naturally, because you've also won the lottery this week. Yes, life keeps getting better.

Running back to your bedroom, you realize what this means. You look down at your partner, who's still asleep in bed, and guess what? Your partner is darn near perfect. Firm body, glowing skin, proportional in every way. The pleasing lover you've always deserved. The thoughtful friend you've always needed. Your partner is your biggest advocate and your toughest, most trusted critic. A voice of intelligence, support, and reason. A life partner par excellence!

You recognize that your entire life, top to bottom, is perfect. Your family is doing well, and they're healthy and relaxed. There's no need for anxiety, frenetic activity, panic, rushing around, or even taking unwanted phone calls.

Your days of throwing down crappy coffee at the office are long *over.* Your dragging ass to the requisite 8:00 a.m. meeting? *Done!* Your taking that client call on your vacation day? *No way!* And guess what? You're never going back to driving your '05 Mercury Mariner, either. That shiny new black BMW 7 Series you always wanted? *It's yours!* And you'll buy it in cash at 1:00 p.m., after you've had a fish pedicure and snail facial.

No more work, no need for more money, and no more worries. Life is whatever you want it to be. Your terms now. Your game. Your rules.

Okay, so that scenario sounds pretty darn great, doesn't it? Breathe it in for a moment.

But then what would you do? Wouldn't you want to know what you had done to wind up in that position? Wouldn't you want to do it again? How do you know you even like that sleeping spouse in the bed? And how will you fill all the empty hours of the day? What if, beyond the surface, deep down you really liked the challenge of showing up, of taking the early meeting, of driving the old clunker, of doing things that tested you, pushed you to solve problems in new ways? What if you liked figuring out how to get more people to buy your new app product, use your design services, acknowledge your contribution to the world?

What if the annoyances and frustrations of the day to day were instead things you could feel grateful for, things that gave you a sense that you had real work to do and were connected to a bigger community of dream owners like you?

Yes, life's difficult, painful at times. It's a process we work through. We know because we're living it, too. As are all those around us. We're hustling to find meaning in our everyday. And yes, it means you have to make choices. And you know what? Work can be an agonizing experience. But there's something interesting that happens to us, something of ineffable value and life-giving energy.

When you dig beyond financial frustrations and debts, rigged games and the social inequities of the world, and listen to enough woe is me, there's a learning and a doing whose value simply can't be replaced or erased, no matter the money. Sometimes the struggles that strain us are the ones that grant us the character for who we are to become. The money will come, that's not the hard part. The hard part is silencing your inner critic and making a conscious psychological commitment to keep going from what is to what could be.

You're going to take licks along the way. Life is more messy than it is clean. Even when you've stashed away more money than you know what to do with and have your name on the front page of the paper, it's still messy. It's still unpredictable. It still requires some degree of risk. It still comes with daily annoyances as you push toward honoring yourself and owning your dream.

The process of going from what you are today to what you are to become takes time. And the truth is, it never ends. That's the mystery and adventure, wrapped neatly together. If it offers consolation, Rome wasn't built in a day, and neither are the best creative minds, the strongest leaders, nor the most innovative companies made in a week or a month. Like fine wine, good things can take time to mature.

Infinite Hustle

Before we bid you adieu, before we let you harvest luck through taking more swings, before you step off the well-worn path to try more oblique approaches, before we watch money and meaning align and combine, before you further your momentum, and before you do something that moves you, keep your head up, eyes open, and seal a deal to make it real, we leave you with our Parthian shot. And we've saved the best for last.

When things go sideways, when no one wants to cooperate with your brilliant ideas, when all your business deals go sour, when your best friend's laughter hurts, when your boyfriend, girlfriend, or spouse leaves you, when your blog doesn't get the traction it deserves, when your job goes wrong, when your new résumé gets zero looks, and when your bank account goes flat broke and you don't have the foggiest notion of how to feed your family . . . remember this: There are only two types of games in the world, finite and infinite.

A finite game always begins and always ends, and it ends when the contestants meet a predetermined condition to define a win or loss. You are already intimately familiar with how a finite game works. A tennis match or a football game make for good examples. In most sports, it means outscoring your opponent in a set time frame. This could be having more runs in nine innings in a baseball game or more goals in four quarters in a water polo game. Furthermore, a finite game always has rules. *Well-defined rules.* The purpose of the rules is to ensure the game ends.

An infinite game has no end and no beginning. The rules are

fluid, and if the rules threaten to make an infinite game finite, the players *must* change them. Sound familiar? Sound like hustle? Never forget: The purpose of the rules in an infinite game is to keep playing.

Keep playing. Never stop your hustling. The point of hustle is not simply money, meaning, and momentum—although you will reap all three. The point is to keep hustling.

We'd wish you luck in your hustle, but you don't need it. You're too busy making your own luck.

ACKNOWLEDGMENTS

Thanks, praise, and shout-outs to the following:

"Consigliere" Scott Hoffman and his team at Folio Literary Agency, which includes Molly Jaffa, Annie Hwang, and others. Sasha Vliet for her research assistance. Our champions at Rodale: Senior editor Ursula Cary, who acquired and believed in this title; senior editor Leah Miller, who did the line editing; editorial assistant, Isabelle Hughes, who calmly kept the production wheels moving; Gail Gonzales, our publisher, and Mary Ann Naples, her predecessor; Angie Giammarino, Melissa Miceli, and Sindy Berner, for leading the charge in our marketing efforts; Yelena Nesbit and Emily Weber Eagan for driving Rodale's publicity efforts. Externally, we thank Mark Fortier and Pamela Peterson of Fortier PR, who helped disseminate our message far and wide; and Tom Morkes and his team at Insurgent Publishing, who helped expand our promotions and partnerships.

Our interviewees, Kelly O'Mara, Fran Hauser, Hugh Forrest, Rebecca Kantar, Ajay Kapoor, Nina Muffleh, Fabrice Grinda, Amit Mathadras, Wendy Papasan, Andrew Kwon, Lewis Katz, and dozens of others. Early advocates like Julia Lord, Ray Bard, and Jay Papasan, and our early readers, including Bijoy Goswami, Neeraj Bansal, Catalina Bravslavski, Claudia "Beluga Love" Fernandez, Stu Galvis, Matt Beaman, and others, for taking time to reflect on our ideas, challenge us, and add to the evolving manuscript. All of our fantastic blurbers, thanks for the read, plug, and assist.

Last, and the opposite of least, we recognize our families. Neil thanks Kiran and Pratima Patel. Patrick thanks Kati, Shane, Milla, and Viola Vlaskovits. Jonas thanks Benjamin Gershman, Judith, Alex, Richard, Robert, Anny, and especially Laura Koffler and Ramses (RIP). You're all part of this enriching journey. We thank you (and anyone we've overlooked) for your support, criticism, love, patience, and so much more.

Further Down the *Hustle* Rabbit Hole:

We found a number of resources edifying or otherwise enlightening in the process of our research and writing. A sampling of the books we recommend you read and videos well worth watching include:

Books

Debt: The First 5,000 Years by David Graeber—Anthropologist David Graeber presents a stunning reversal of conventional wisdom: He shows that before there was money, there was debt. For more than 5,000 years, since the beginnings of the first agrarian empires, humans have used elaborate credit systems to buy and sell goods—that is, long before the invention of coins or cash. It is in this era, Graeber argues, that we also first encounter a society divided into debtors and creditors.

Chase, Chance, and Creativity: The Lucky Art of Novelty by James H. Austin, MD—This first book by the author of *Zen and the Brain* examines the role of chance in the creative process. Austin tells a personal story of the ways in which persistence, chance, and creativity interact in biomedical research; the conclusions he reaches shed light on the creative process in any field. He shows how, in his own investigations, unpredictable events shaped the outcome of his research and brought about novel results.

The Little Prince by Antoine de Saint-Exupéry—After being stranded in a desert following a crash, a pilot comes in contact with a captivating little prince who recounts his journey from planet to planet and his search for what is most important in life.

Stumbling on Happiness by Dan Gilbert—In this brilliant, witty, and accessible book, renowned Harvard psychologist Daniel Gilbert describes the foibles of imagination and illusions of foresight that cause each of us to misconceive our tomorrows and misestimate our satisfactions. Vividly bringing to life the latest scientific research in psychology, cognitive neuroscience, philosophy, and behavioral economics, Gilbert reveals what scientists have discovered about the uniquely human ability to imagine the future and about our capacity to predict how much we will like it when we get there.

Decisive: How to Make Better Choices in Life and Work by Chip and Dan
Heath—Chip and Dan Heath, the bestselling authors of *Switch* and *Made
to Stick,* tackle one of the most critical topics in our work and personal lives:
how to make better decisions.

*Year of Yes: How to Dance It Out, Stand In the Sun and Be Your Own
Person* by Shonda Rhimes—In this poignant, hilarious, and deeply intimate
call to arms, Hollywood's most powerful woman, the mega-talented creator of
Grey's Anatomy and *Scandal* and executive producer of *How to Get Away with
Murder* reveals how saying YES changed her life—and how it can change
yours too.

Managing Oneself by Peter F. Drucker—We live in an age of unprecedented
opportunity: with ambition, drive, and talent, you can rise to the top of your
chosen profession regardless of where you started out. But with opportunity
comes responsibility. Companies today aren't managing their knowledge
workers' careers. Instead, you must be your own chief executive officer.

Self-Renewal: The Individual and the Innovative Society by John W.
Gardner—In his classic treatise, Gardner examines why great societies
thrive and die. He argues that it is dynamism not decay that is dramatically
altering the landscape of American society. The 20th century has brought
about change more rapidly than any previous era, and with that came
advancements, challenges, and often destruction. Gardner cautions that "a
society must court the kinds of change that will enrich and strengthen it
rather than the kind of change that will fragment and destroy it."

Learned Optimism: How to Change Your Mind and Your Life by Martin
E. P. Seligman, PhD—Known as the father of the new science of positive
psychology, Seligman draws on more than 20 years of clinical research to
demonstrate how optimism enhances the quality of life and how anyone can
learn to practice it.

Obliquity: Why Our Goals Are Best Achieved Indirectly by John Kay—In
this revolutionary book, economist John Kay proves a notion that feels at
once paradoxical and deeply commonsensical: The best way to achieve any
complex or broadly defined goal, from happiness to preventing forest fires, is
the indirect way.

How to Fail at Almost Everything and Still Win Big by Scott Adams—
Dilbert creator Scott Adams offers his most personal book ever—a funny
memoir of his many failures and what they eventually taught him about
success. How do you go from hapless office worker to world-famous cartoonist
and bestselling author in just a few years? No career guide can answer that,
and not even Scott Adams (who actually did it) can give you a road map that
works for everyone. But there's a lot to learn from his personal story, and a lot
of humor along the way.

Finite and Infinite Games: A Vision of Life as Play and Possibility by
James P. Carse—What are infinite games? How do they affect the ways

we play our finite games? What are we doing when we play—finitely or infinitely? And how can infinite games affect the ways in which we live our lives? Carse explores these questions with stunning elegance, teasing out of his distinctions a universe of observation and insight, noting where and why and how we play, finitely and infinitely. He surveys our world—from the finite games of the playing field and playing board to the infinite games found in culture and religion—leaving all we think we know illuminated and transformed.

Time Enough for Love by Robert A. Heinlein—The capstone and crowning achievement of Heinlein's famous Future History, *Time Enough for Love* follows Lazarus Long through a vast and magnificent timescape of centuries and worlds. Heinlein's longest and most ambitious work, it is the story of a man so in love with Life that he refused to stop living it; and so in love with Time that he became his own ancestor.

The War of Art: Break Through the Blocks and Win Your Inner Creative Battles by Steven Pressfield—What keeps so many of us from doing what we long to do? Why is there a naysayer within? How can we avoid the roadblocks of any creative endeavor—be it starting up a dream business venture, writing a novel, or painting a masterpiece? Bestselling novelist Steven Pressfield identifies the enemy that every one of us must face, outlines a battle plan to conquer this internal foe, then pinpoints just how to achieve the greatest success.

Conversations with Picasso by Brassaï—This book offers a remarkable vision of both Picasso and the entire artistic and intellectual milieu of wartime Paris, a vision provided by the gifted photographer and prolific author who spent the early portion of the 1940s photographing Picasso's work. Brassaï carefully and affectionately records each of his meetings and appointments with the great artist, building along the way a work of remarkable depth, intimate perspective, and great importance to anyone who truly wishes to understand Picasso and his world.

The Lean Entrepreneur by Brant Cooper and Patrick Vlaskovits—The *New York Times* bestseller banishes the "Myth of the Visionary" and shows you how you can implement proven, actionable techniques to create products and disrupt existing markets on your way to entrepreneurial success. This great guide combines the concepts of customer insight, rapid experimentation, and actionable data from the Lean Startup methodology to allow individuals, teams, or even entire companies to solve problems, create value, and ramp up their vision quickly and efficiently.

Art and Artist: Creative Urge and Personality Development by Otto Rank— *Art and Artist* explores the human urge to create in all its complex aspects, in terms not only of individual works of art but of religion, mythology, and social institutions as well. Based firmly on Rank's knowledge of psychology and psychoanalysis, it ranges widely through anthropology and cultural history, reaching beyond psychology to a broad understanding of human nature.

Pitch Anything: An Innovative Method for Presenting, Persuading, and Winning the Deal by Oren Klaff—When it comes to delivering a pitch, Klaff has unparalleled credentials. Over the past 13 years, he has used his one-of-a-kind method to raise more than $400 million—and now, for the first time, he describes his formula to help you deliver a winning pitch in any business situation. Whether you're selling ideas to investors, pitching a client for new business, or even negotiating for a higher salary, *Pitch Anything* will transform the way you position your ideas.

Grit: The Power of Passion and Perseverance by Angela Duckworth— Pioneering psychologist Angela Duckworth shows anyone striving to succeed—be it parents, students, educators, athletes, or business people— that the secret to outstanding achievement is not talent but a special blend of passion and persistence she calls "grit."

Outliers: The Story of Success by Malcolm Gladwell—Gladwell argues that if we want to understand how some people thrive, we should spend more time looking *around* them, at such things as their family, their birthplace, or even their birth date. And in revealing that hidden logic, Gladwell presents a fascinating and provocative blueprint for making the most of human potential.

Greatness: Who Makes History and Why by Dean Keith Simonton, PhD— What do Madonna, Confucius, and Jackie Robinson have in common? What does it take to go down in history as a great political leader? Why do revolutions occur, riots break out, and lynch mobs assemble? Which events do people find the most shocking or memorable? This path-breaking work offers the first comprehensive examination of the important personalities and events that have influenced the course of history. It discusses whether people who go down in history are different from the rest of us; whether specific personality traits predispose certain people to become world leaders, movie stars, scientific geniuses, and athletes, while others are relegated to ordinary lives. In exploring the psychology of greatness, this volume sheds light on the characteristics that any of us may share with history-making people.

Deceit and Self-Deception: Fooling Yourself the Better to Fool Others by Robert Trivers—Acclaimed by figures such as Richard Dawkins and Steven Pinker, Trivers looks at how and why we so often deceive ourselves. We lie to ourselves every day: about how well we drive, how much we're enjoying ourselves—even how good-looking we are. In this groundbreaking book, Robert Trivers examines not only how we self-deceive but also why—taking fascinating examples from aviation disasters, con artists, sexual betrayals and conflicts within families. Revealing, provocative, and witty, *Deceit and Self-Deception* is one of the most vital books written this century and will make you rethink everything that you think you know.

Power Cues: The Subtle Science of Leading Groups, Persuading Others, and Maximizing Your Personal Impact by Nick Morgan—What if someone told you that your behavior was controlled by a powerful, invisible force? Most of us would be skeptical of such a claim—but it's largely true. Our brains are constantly transmitting and receiving signals of which we are unaware. Studies show that these constant inputs drive the great majority of our decisions about what to do next—and we become conscious of the decisions only after we start acting on them. Many may find that disturbing. But the implications for leadership are profound. In this provocative yet practical book, renowned speaking coach and communication expert Nick Morgan highlights recent research that shows how humans are programmed to respond to the nonverbal cues of others—subtle gestures, sounds, and signals—that elicit emotion.

Videos

George Carlin, "The American Dream" YouTube video, 3:00, last accessed June 20, 2016, https://www.youtube.com/watch?v=rsL6mKxtOlQ. Bitly.com/ GeorgeCarlinAmericanDream

Shonda Rhimes, "Be a Doer, Not a Dreamer" during 2014 Dartmouth commencement speech, YouTube video, 24:00, last accessed June 20, 2016, https://www.youtube.com/watch?v=EuHQ6TH60_I, http://bit.ly/BeADoer

Louis CK, "Everything Is Amazing and Nobody Is Happy," YouTube video, 4:13, last accessed June 20, 2016, https://www.youtube.com/ watch?v=q8LaT5Iiwo4, Bitly.com/EverythingIsAmazing

Ira Glass from *This American Life*, "Storytelling: Part 1 of 4," YouTube video, 5:23, last accessed June 20, 2016, https://www.youtube.com/watch?v=loxJ3FtCJJA, Bitly.com/IraGlassStory

ENDNOTES

Chapter 1

1 www.iop.harvard.edu/harvard-iop-fall-2015-poll

2 http://usnews.nbcnews.com/_news/2013/04/24/17882085-americans-head-north-for-affordable-college-degrees?lite

3 http://www.smh.com.au/business/the-economy/australian-households-awash-with-debt-barclays-20150315-1lzyz4.html

Chapter 2

1 www.healthyhorns.utexas.edu/n_dietsoda.html

2 http://www.purdue.edu/uns/x/2008a/080211SwithersAPA.html

Chapter 11

1 David Obstfeld, "Social Networks, the *Tertius Iungens* Orientation, and Involvement in Innovation," *Administrative Science Quarterly* 50, no. 1 (March 2005): 100–130.

This book has covered a lot of conceptual ground. Here's a glossary to understand the key concepts in *Hustle*.

10-Minute Rule: To destroy procrastination, begin attacking any specific task with only a 10-minute commitment of your time. Then pull your head up out of the task and review if you want to keep going. Most of the time, you'll find that you just needed to get beyond the initial inertia.

Use the 10-Minute Rule for tackling everything from your work to exercise, creative projects, reading—whatever. Just do it. And repeat.

ABCs: In sales, the ABC mantra refers to "A=Always, B=Be, C=Closing." If you're unclear, watch Alec Baldwin's character in the film *Glengarry Glen Ross*. When it comes to Hustle, and specifically in cultivating the People piece of your POP, "ABCs" means

A = Always, B = Be, Cs = Collaborating & Connecting

When you meet someone new, just ask yourself: What's in it for them?

Allenism: An Allenism is any skill or habit that gives you an advantage just by the virtue of doing it. Mastery is not required.

Cycle of Suck: A repetitive cyclical form of learned helplessness. When we're in a Cycle of Suck, we're dispirited and incapable of moving toward a goal. Moreover, we cannot help ourselves to break the cycle and every action we take only exacerbates our situation. Cycles of Suck are insidious because they subconsciously lower our expectations about what we can achieve and get out of life.

Eurocratese: The unofficial language spoken by all European bureaucrats and politicians. It has a melodic quality but understanding meaning and intent is difficult.

ESP: An acronym for Experimentation, Storytelling, Persuasion. The core Allenisms that any and every Hustler should learn.

The Fourfold Path: A set of four fundamental career moves–each a distinct course of action of its own making–designed to liberate you and enable you to grow through new opportunities in your pursuit of fulfilling work. Each of the four pathways operates with a high degree of predictability and repeatability. And just like with obliquity, the path forward implies movement not in a straight line, but instead in an adventurous route that leads up, down, and sideways, ultimately pulling you from what you are to what you will become.

The Fourfold Path includes:

1. The Outside/Inside Hustle–the proverbial 'foot in the door' of a new company or gig
2. The Inside/Upside Hustle–promotion should you choose to ascend the corporate ladder
3. The Inside/ Outside Hustle–movement from one organization to another or toward entrepreneurial endeavors
4. The Outside/Upside Hustle–movement that accelerates toward large-scale and often epic entrepreneurial achievements

Hidden Luck: One of the four types of luck as described by Dr. James Austin. Hidden luck is manufactured by learning to see the hidden patterns right in front of us.

Hustle Generation: The group of people who have decided to eschew "playing by the rules" of social convention and who know that movement towards a goal, however indirect, pays off in money, meaning, and momentum.

Hustle Luck: One of the four types of luck as described by Dr. James Austin. Hustle luck is created by motion, seeing things from a new vantage point and stirring things up.

Hustle: A decisive movement toward a goal, however indirect, by which the motion itself manufactures luck, surfaces hidden opportunities, and charges our lives with more money, meaning, and momentum.

Infinite Hustle: A reference to the work of James Carse. 'Infinite games' are games where we must change the rules if they threaten to stop play. The point of the game is to keep playing. Likewise, the point of hustling is to keep hustling.

Kangaroo Court of Talents: Kangaroo courts are courts that do not seek justice, but rather public humiliation and scapegoating. When we ask others to judge our innate talents, we often get unhelpful feedback that only demoralizes us. One of the psychological traps that lead to the Risk of Learned Blindness.

Lake Wobegon Effect: The tendency to protect our fragile egos by lying to ourselves that we are better at some skill or activity than we are. Another of the psychological traps that makes us blind to our real talents.

Landlords: The people and institutions that force us on the paths that they own so they can tax us when we pass by and hinder our hustle. They want us to rent dreams from them, and forget about owning our own dreams.

Madness of Mastery: When mastery of a skill itself becomes the goal of skill acquisition we confuse the target with the trophy. The target, what we want to accomplish with the skill, should always be the target. Do you want to win a storytelling contest (trophy) or do you want to tell a story that closes a million dollar deal (target)?

Mediocrity of Meh: We're in stasis. Not moving. Life is grey. We're not succeeding, yet we're not failing, and as such, we're too complacent to change our behavior. And there is a nagging feeling that we're missing out on something. Our subconscious isn't wrong, we are.

Obliquity: The principle that often the indirect route is the best route to accomplish our goals. This is especially true if we are doing something off-kilter, novel or weird.

Owning a Dream: As opposed to 'Renting a Dream', owning a dream means actively choosing to choose your dream. You capture the upside of ownership and own up to the responsibilities of making it happen. Not just sitting around wishing or dreaming a dream. The best way to realize more money, meaning, and momentum.

People Leverage: The principle that you need not lone wolf your way through life, trying to know everything or accomplish everything alone. The truth is that someone else has already solved whatever problem you have. You can apply the 10-Minute Rule to decide whether you have the expertise to solve a particular problem alone or if you must find someone else to assist you. In a way, this is how you can compress Gladwell's exalted 10,000-Hours Rule into...get this, a 10-minute decision. Bring on somebody else to lend a mind or a hand. Save yourself the hassle, git 'er done.

Perils of Perfection: For most people (including your authors), perfectionism is a major obstacle to getting stuff done. Perfectionism is a dangerous bogeyman that prevents us from helping ourselves. Nothing is ever perfect yet 'great artists ship' noted Steve Jobs. Don't let perfect be the enemy of good.

POP: The Personal Opportunity Portfolio or POP is a diversified basket of value and right-sized risk you create through your pursuits of Potential, People, Projects and Proof pieces.

POP Chart: A visual arrangement that maps to each of the four key pieces of your Personal Opportunity Portfolio: Potential, People, Projects and Proof.

Proofbergs: How you prove to yourself and others that you are capable of creation.

Quirky Luck: A product of Hustle Luck and Hidden Luck. How eccentric and weird people see the same thing as the rest of us, and come to different conclusions about its nature. If you're naturally funky or odd, embrace it. You'll get luckier.

Random Luck: One of the four types of luck. What most people perceive as the accidental or chance kind of luck.

Renting a Dream: Following a pre-described, standard script for happiness, success and meaning, designed to benefit not you, but those who have handed you the script.

Risk of Learned Blindness: The risk that defines our entire life. That we learn to be blind to what we were meant to do or what we were meant to become.

Self-Diagnosing Talent Exercise: The best way to learn about who we are and what we are meant to do. By trying new projects and marking down our results over time, we can self-diagnose what our strengths and talents are. Doing just that will prevent us from being judged at a Kangaroo Court of Talents of our peers as well as short-circuit the Lake Wobegon effect.

Swing Theory: Based on Dean Keith Simonton's work. The observation that life isn't like a baseball game. You can get up to bat as often as you like and striking out doesn't really matter.

Tertius Iungens & Tertius Gaudens: Based on the work of David Obstfeld. Tertius iungens is the "the third who joins". TIs are social information brokers who help coordinate action and introduce two (or more) parties to one another to foster collaboration. See ABCs.

Tertius Gaudens is the "third who benefits." TGs are classic middlemen who benefit from information gaps or conflicts between two parties.

The Fun House Mirrors of Talent Perception: Fun house mirrors distort our reflections. The Lake Wobegon effect and The Kangaroo Court of Talents distort our perceptions of our talents.

The More Effect: Money needs meaning as much as meaning needs money. The two have a tightly coupled relationship. If one gets out of balance in proportion to the other, we feel a nagging feeling of more. See Mediocrity of Meh.

Three Unseen Laws of Hustle:

1. Do Something That Moves You.
   Something that moves you physically. This way you can leverage Hustle Luck (the luck created by movement), and engage your heart in deciding your next course of action.
2. Keep Your Head Up and Your Eyes Open.
   Now you're moving and doing something. Your movement will generate the effect of having you see the world in novel ways. Seeing the world in new ways will surface previously hidden opportunities to you.
3. Seal the Deal and Make It Real.

Talk Is Cheap: When you see an opportunity, create and close a transaction. The transaction doesn't have to be huge—a small one will do. You need the closure of a transaction to get your breath and keep moving.

Your Real Why: Our motivations are mostly hidden from ourselves, which is why 'figuring out your why' is mostly nonsense. The only way we can figure out 'our real why' is by taking on challenging projects and observing our own behavior over time. See Self-Diagnosing Talent Exercise.

INDEX

Boldface page references indicate illustrations. Underscored references indicate tables or boxed text.

ABOUT THE AUTHORS

NEIL PATEL is the cofounder of Crazy Egg and Hello Bar. He helps companies like NBC, GM, HP, and Viacom grow their revenue. The *Wall Street Journal* calls him a top influencer on the Web, *Forbes* says he is one of the top 10 online marketers, and *Entrepreneur* says he created one of the 100 most brilliant companies in the world. Tweet him **@NeilPatel** or contact him by visiting NeilPatel.com.

PATRICK VLASKOVITS is an entrepreneur and *New York Times* bestselling author. His writing has been featured in the *Harvard Business Review* and the *Wall Street Journal*, and he speaks at technology conferences nationally and internationally, including SXSW, GROW conference, the Turing Festival, and the Lean Startup conference. He is cofounder and CEO of Superpowered Inc. Tweet him **@Pv** or contact him by visiting Vlaskovits.com.

JONAS KOFFLER is a creative media consultant, producer, and writer. He advises internationally recognized thought leaders and creative artists, helps organizations innovate, develops strategy and intellectual property for start-ups and billion-dollar companies alike, and has contributed to multiple bestselling books. Tweet him **@JonasKoffler** or contact him by visiting JonasKoffler.com.

And be sure to visit **HustleGeneration.com** for:

- Free tools and online resources designed for our readers.
- News, interviews, events, and updates on the book.
- Innovation, education, and empowerment training.
- Giveaways, special offers, and more…